ST. LU
TRAVEL (
2025

A New Pocket Manual for Discovering Top Beaches, Local Food Spots, and Must-See Attractions with Maps, Pictures, and Itineraries for an Unforgettable Island Adventure

Albert N. Allred

Copyright © 2024 (Albert N. Allred)

All rights reserved. No part of this book may be reproduced or transmitted in any form or by any means, electronic or mechanical, including photocopying, recording or by any information storage and retrieval system, without written permission from the author, except for the inclusion of brief quotations embodied in critical reviews and certain other non commercial uses permitted by copyright law.

Disclaimer

Welcome to Your **St. Lucia Travel Guide 2025!** Get ready to discover the island paradise of St. Lucia with this comprehensive guide, packed with local insights and must-visit spots. From the iconic Pitons to the crystal-clear waters of the Caribbean, we'll help you experience the true beauty of St. Lucia.

Remember that island life can bring unexpected changes to prices, hours, and tour schedules. To ensure a smooth trip, be sure to confirm key details with your hotels, tour operators, and attractions before you set off.

Think of this guide as your St. Lucian companion, guiding you to memorable adventures and hidden gems. With a bit of preparation, your journey to this tropical haven will be everything you've dreamed of.

Enjoy your travels!

Table of Contents

Introduction 7
Chapter 1: Welcome to St. Lucia 10
    A. A Brief History 10
    B. Why Visit St. Lucia in 2025? 13
    C. Geography and Climate 14
Chapter 2: Travel Essentials 17
    A. Best Time to Visit St. Lucia 17
    B. Entry Requirements and Visas ... 19
    C. Currency, Budget, and Costs 21
    D. Health and Safety Tips 24
    E. Language and Local Etiquette 26
Chapter 3: Getting to and Around St. Lucia 32
    A. Flights and Arrival: Airports Overview 32
    B. Transportation Options: Taxis, Buses, and Car Rentals 36
    C. Island Hopping and Day Trips 40
Chapter 4: Accommodations for Every

Budget..............................44
  A. Top Luxury Resorts...................44
  B. Mid-Range Hotels and Boutique Stays.................................49
  C. Budget-Friendly Options and Hostels..................................54
Chapter 5: Itinerary Planning............59
  A. Sample 3-Day Itinerary............... 59
  B. Sample 5-Day Itinerary...............63
  C. Sample 7-Day Itinerary...............68
  D. Tips for Customizing Your Trip....73
Chapter 6: Top Attractions and Must-See Sights........................ 79
  A. The Pitons................................79
  B. Soufrière Volcano and Sulphur Springs..................................83
  C. Pigeon Island National Park........88
  D. Diamond Falls and Botanical Gardens.................................91
  E. Castries Market and Local Experiences............................96
Chapter 7: Beaches of St. Lucia........100

    A. The Best Beaches for Relaxation... 100

    B. Snorkeling and Diving Spots.... 104

    C. Hidden Gems................................ 110

Chapter 8: Outdoor Adventures and Activities... 115

    A. Hiking and Nature Trails............ 115

    B. Water Sports................................ 120

    C. Snorkeling and Scuba Diving... 125

    D. Zip-Lining and Aerial Adventures: Soar Above St. Lucia's Rainforest Canopy... 130

    E. Whale Watching and Dolphin Tours.. 136

Chapter 9: Cultural Experiences...... 142

    A. Festivals and Events in 2025... 142

    B. Music, Dance, and Local Art..... 146

    C. Exploring St. Lucian Cuisine..... 150

    D. Museums and Historical Sites.. 154

Chapter 10: St. Lucian Food and Drink. 160

A. Must-Try Dishes and Street Food... 160

B. Top Restaurants and Cafés....... 164

C. Best Local Bars and Nightlife... 169

Chapter 11: Shopping and Souvenirs.... 175

A. Local Markets and Artisan Shops... 175

B. Best Places to Buy Souvenirs... 180

C. Tips for Bargaining and Finding Authentic Goods............................ 185

Chapter 12: Family Travel in St. Lucia... 190

A. Kid-Friendly Attractions and Activities.................................... 190

B. Family-Friendly Accommodations.. 194

C. Safety Tips for Traveling with Children............................... 199

Chapter 13: Travel Tips and Resources 205

A. Travel Apps and Online Resources

205

B. Packing Tips for St. Lucia............ 210

C. Staying Connected....................... 214

D. Emergency Contacts and Useful Numbers... 218

Conclusion... 222

Bonus: Authentic St. Lucian Recipes..... 226

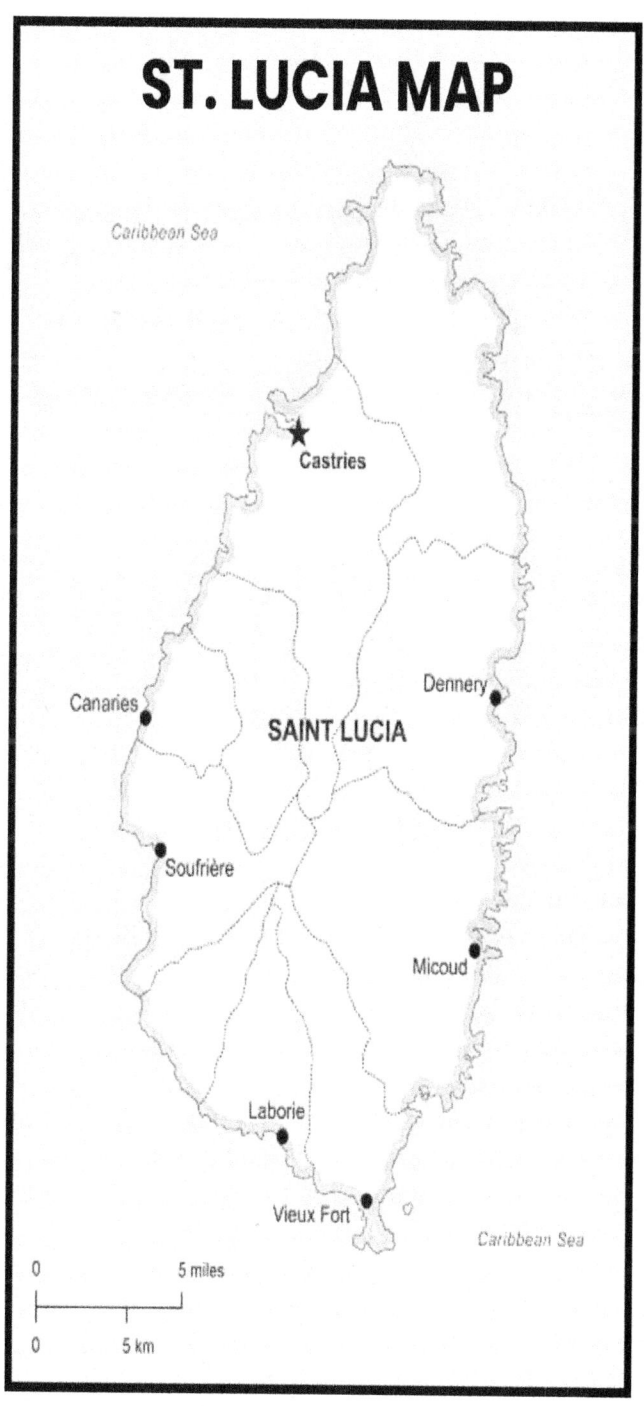

Introduction

Hey there, fellow explorers!

So, you're thinking about St. Lucia, huh? Brilliant choice! This island isn't just another Caribbean destination; it's a place that gets under your skin and fills you with a sense of wonder. I've had the joy of visiting St. Lucia many times, and every single trip feels like an invitation to uncover new stories, breathtaking landscapes, and hidden corners of paradise.

Let me tell you about my most recent adventure in 2024—it was like the island decided to show me its best-kept secrets. One of those unforgettable moments was stumbling across Anse La Raye on a quiet morning. The sun was rising, casting a golden glow over the fishing boats bobbing in the bay. I ended up chatting with a local fisherman who shared stories of his family's deep connection to the sea. Moments like these make you realize there's more to this place than just what you see on postcards.

And then there was the time I hiked up Gros Piton. It's not an easy trek, but reaching the summit was worth every drop of sweat. Standing there, looking out at the sweeping views of the island and the endless blue of the ocean, I felt like I'd found my own little piece of heaven. If you're up for the challenge, this hike will give you one of the most spectacular panoramas you could ever imagine.

I also have to tell you about snorkeling at Anse Chastanet. The water was so clear, it was like swimming in a giant, colorful aquarium. I floated alongside vibrant fish, and at one point, a sea turtle glided right past me. It felt like time had stopped, and it was just me, the coral, and the gentle rhythm of the waves. If you're into snorkeling or diving, this spot is an absolute must.

But it wasn't just the natural beauty that made my trip so special—it was the people. Like the time I joined a cooking class in Soufrière and learned how to make green fig and saltfish, the island's national dish. The chef, a St. Lucian grandmother with a warm smile, shared stories about her childhood and how food has always brought her family together. Or the evening I spent at a street party in Gros Islet, dancing to soca music under the stars and sampling the best grilled chicken I've ever had.

These are the experiences that make St. Lucia more than just a destination—they make it a place you carry with you long after you leave. It's a mix of stunning scenery, vibrant culture, and unforgettable connections that you just can't get anywhere else.

So, what are you waiting for? Dive into this guide, start planning your own adventure, and get ready to create memories you'll treasure for a lifetime. Who knows, maybe we'll cross paths on the beach or at a local rum shack. Until then, happy travels, and welcome to the magic of St. Lucia!

Chapter 1: Welcome to St. Lucia

A. A Brief History

Let's go back in time, way before cruise ships and beach resorts, to when St. Lucia was a wild, untouched island in the middle of the Caribbean Sea. The first people to live here were the Arawak, a peaceful group who arrived around 200 AD. They sailed from South America, bringing with them the skills to fish, farm, and craft pottery. They called the island "Iouanalao," which means "Island of the Iguanas." And you guessed it—they picked that name because iguanas were everywhere!

But the Arawak didn't stay the rulers of the island for long. Around 800 AD, the Carib people showed up. They were tougher and more warlike, pushing the Arawak out and renaming the island "Hewanorra." These were the days of small villages, canoes carved from trees, and a deep connection to the land and sea. The Caribs were great sailors, and their culture thrived here for centuries.

Then, in the late 1400s, everything changed. European explorers were sailing the seas, searching for new lands, and it wasn't long before they spotted St. Lucia. Legend has it that Christopher Columbus may have glimpsed the island on his final voyage in 1502, but it was really the French and British who became obsessed with it in the 1600s. Why? Because St. Lucia was like a treasure chest—fertile land, fresh water, and a perfect location in the Caribbean. The French were the first to set up camp in 1650, but it wasn't easy. The Caribs didn't exactly roll out the welcome mat, and the French settlers faced fierce resistance.

What happened next was like a never-ending game of tug-of-war. Over the next 150 years, St. Lucia switched hands between the French and British 14 times! Imagine how confusing that must have been for the people living here—one day they were ruled by France, the next by Britain. This back-and-forth is why St. Lucia got the nickname "Helen of the West Indies," comparing the island to Helen of Troy, the woman fought over by ancient empires.

Finally, in 1814, the British took control for good, but by then, the island's identity was a unique mix of cultures. The French influence lingered, especially in the local Creole language (Kwéyòl) and delicious food like bouyon and accras. Meanwhile, the British brought new systems of law and government.

The 19th century saw the end of slavery in St. Lucia, a huge turning point in its history. Freed African slaves began to shape the island's culture even more, blending their traditions with European influences to create something uniquely St. Lucian. Fast forward to the 20th century, and the island was ready for change. In 1967, St. Lucia gained control over its own government as an associated state of the United Kingdom. Then, on February 22, 1979, the island celebrated full independence, becoming a sovereign nation for the first time.

Today, St. Lucia's history is everywhere you look—from the Pigeon Island National Park, where you can explore old military forts, to the lively streets of Castries, where you'll hear the rhythms of soca and reggae blending with the chatter in Creole. It's a place where the past meets the present, where you can taste the French influence in a bite of freshly baked breadfruit pie or feel the African heritage in the beat of a traditional drum dance.

St. Lucia's history is one of strength and adaptation. It's about a small island that was fought over and colonized, but never lost its soul.

Today, it stands as a proud, independent nation, rich in culture, history, and the warm spirit of its people. As you explore the island, remember—you're walking through centuries of stories, woven into every hill, beach, and village. Enjoy uncovering them!

B. Why Visit St. Lucia in 2025?

The year 2025 is your year to make it happen. St. Lucia isn't just another Caribbean island—it's the one that sticks with you long after you leave.

Why now? Well, 2025 is packed with new surprises. The island is buzzing with fresh energy, from boutique hotels popping up in hidden spots to eco-friendly tours that take you off the beaten path. Whether you're chilling on the soft sands of Sugar Beach or catching the sunset over the iconic Pitons, St. Lucia knows how to deliver those picture-perfect moments you've been craving.

Let's talk weather (because we all love sunshine, right?). St. Lucia enjoys warm, sunny days pretty much year-round. Expect temps around 80°F (27°C) with a lovely breeze to keep things comfy. Sure, you might get a quick shower, especially between June and November, but they're the kind that disappear just as fast as they come, leaving the air fresh and the island even greener.

But it's not just about beaches. St. Lucia is alive with culture, music, and festivals that you'll want to dive right into. Plan your trip around the St. Lucia Jazz Festival for live music and dancing under the stars, or visit during Carnival, where the streets come alive with costumes, parades, and that infectious island vibe.

And the food? Oh, you're in for a treat! From the national dish, green fig and saltfish, to spicy Creole street food, your taste buds are in for an adventure of their own. Swing by the Castries Market for a local bite, or grab a beachside rum punch as you soak up the sunset.

C. Geography and Climate

Alright, let's get you oriented! St. Lucia may be a small island, but it's big on personality and packed with jaw-dropping scenery. Picture this: lush rainforests, dramatic volcanic peaks, and some of the bluest waters you'll ever see. If you love exploring, this island is basically a giant playground.

Where is St. Lucia?
St. Lucia is hanging out in the eastern Caribbean, right between Martinique and St. Vincent. It's part of the Windward Islands, and it's shaped a bit like a mango (we're not kidding!). The island stretches about 27 miles (43 km) long and 14 miles (23 km) wide, which means you can easily explore from top to bottom in a day—if you're up for a road trip. But trust us, you'll want to take it slow and enjoy every stop along the way.

The star of the show? It's got to be the Pitons—those two towering volcanic peaks, Gros Piton and Petit Piton. They're like nature's skyscrapers, rising straight out of the ocean and giving the island its iconic silhouette. Whether you're hiking up Gros Piton or just gazing at them from the beach, these giants are a sight you won't forget.

Let's Talk Weather
Sunshine, anyone? St. Lucia's tropical climate means warm, sunny days almost all year round. You're looking at average temperatures between 77°F and 86°F (25°C to 30°C), so pack your sunscreen and get ready to soak up those rays. And the best part? There's a lovely breeze from the trade winds that keeps things feeling fresh, especially along the coast.

The island has two main seasons: the dry season (December to May) and the wet season (June to

November). Don't stress about the wet season, though. Rain showers are usually quick and leave the air smelling like fresh flowers. Plus, they turn the island into a lush, green paradise—perfect for those epic Instagram photos.

What's the Landscape Like?
Beyond the beaches, St. Lucia's terrain is full of surprises. You've got rolling hills, dense rainforests, and even a drive-in volcano (yes, you read that right). Head to the Sulphur Springs near Soufrière for a chance to soak in the hot springs or take a mud bath—it's nature's spa treatment, and your skin will thank you.

On the east coast, the Atlantic Ocean brings waves and rugged cliffs, perfect for adventurous surfers. Meanwhile, the west coast faces the calm, crystal-clear Caribbean Sea, where you'll find perfect spots for snorkeling and swimming.

Chapter 2: Travel Essentials

A. Best Time to Visit St. Lucia

Alright, let's get down to business—when is the best time to visit this tropical paradise? Truth is, there's no bad time to come to St. Lucia, but depending on what kind of experience you're looking for, certain months might suit you better.

The Dry Season (December to May):

This is hands down the most popular time to visit St. Lucia. Why? Because the weather is perfect—plenty of sunshine, clear skies, and very little rain. Temperatures hover around 77°F to 86°F (25°C to 30°C), making it ideal for beach days, hiking, and exploring the island's many attractions. It's also when you'll find the island at its liveliest, with major events like the St. Lucia Jazz Festival happening in May. Just keep in mind that this is peak tourist season, so expect higher prices and book your accommodation early if you're planning a winter getaway.

The Wet Season (June to November):

Don't let the name scare you off—the wet season in St. Lucia isn't as rainy as it sounds. Yes, you'll get the occasional tropical shower, but they're usually quick and followed by sunny skies. Plus, the rain brings out the island's lush greenery, making it a great time for nature lovers. Temperatures are warm, ranging from 79°F to 88°F (26°C to 31°C), and the ocean is perfect for swimming. Another bonus? It's the low season, so you can score some great deals on hotels and tours. Just keep an eye on the weather forecast during the hurricane season (August to October), although St. Lucia typically avoids the worst of the storms.

Best Time for Specific Activities:

- Beach and Sunbathing: Anytime is a good time, but December to May offers the sunniest days.
- Hiking the Pitons: Aim for the dry season for the best conditions and clear views from the top.
- Snorkeling and Diving: The waters are clearest from February to April, perfect for spotting colorful fish and coral reefs.

- Local Festivals: Visit in July for Carnival, a vibrant celebration full of parades, music, and dancing.

Quick Tips:

- If you're visiting during the dry season, bring a light jacket for cooler evenings, especially if you plan to hike in the mountains.
- During the wet season, pack a travel umbrella or rain jacket—showers can be brief but intense.
- For those traveling in the off-season, take advantage of lower prices and enjoy the island without the crowds.

B. Entry Requirements and Visas

Let's make sure you know exactly what you need so you can breeze through immigration and get straight to enjoying your island adventure.

Who Needs a Visa?

If you're traveling from the United States, Canada, the United Kingdom, or most European countries, you're in luck—no visa is required for visits up to 6 weeks. All you need is a valid passport that's good for at least 6 months beyond your travel date. Easy, right? For travelers from countries that do require a visa, it's a simple process to apply online or through a St. Lucian embassy. Be sure to check the latest visa requirements based on your nationality before booking your trip.

Essential Documents:

Here's what you'll need when you arrive:
- A valid passport (with at least 6 months of validity left)
- Proof of onward travel (like a return flight ticket)
- Proof of accommodation, such as a hotel booking confirmation
- Health documents (if required), especially if you're traveling from a region with certain health concerns

Health and Safety Measures:

Since the global pandemic, travel protocols can change quickly, so it's a good idea to keep an eye on St. Lucia's official tourism website for any updates. As of now, most restrictions have eased, but it's wise to have a copy of your COVID-19 vaccination certificate or a recent negative test result just in case. Health protocols might still apply at certain venues or events.

Customs and What You Can Bring In:

St. Lucia is pretty relaxed, but there are still a few things you should know about customs regulations:
- You can bring personal items and duty-free goods, like 1 liter of alcohol and 200 cigarettes (if you smoke).
- If you're traveling with expensive gadgets, like cameras or drones, be sure to declare them.
- Don't bring any illegal substances or restricted items, as St. Lucia has strict drug laws.

Arrival Tips:

When you land at Hewanorra International Airport (UVF) or George F.L. Charles Airport (SLU), you'll go through immigration first. The lines can be a bit long during peak travel times, so be patient and have your documents ready. The officers are friendly and might even give you some local tips on where to go and what to see!

A Quick Heads-Up:

Make sure to have a little cash on hand (Eastern Caribbean Dollars or USD) for any small fees or tips at the airport. Most places on the island accept major credit cards, but it's always handy to have some cash, especially for taxis or small purchases.

C. Currency, Budget, and Costs

Here's the lowdown on what you need to know about money on the island.

What's the Currency?
St. Lucia uses the Eastern Caribbean Dollar (EC$), but don't worry if you have U.S. dollars (USD) because they're widely accepted too. The exchange rate hovers around EC$2.70 for $1 USD, but it's good to double-check before you travel. Most places will accept major credit cards like Visa and Mastercard, especially in hotels, restaurants, and tourist shops. It's always a good idea to carry some local cash, though, especially if you plan to visit small markets or take a local taxi.

How Much Should You Budget?
St. Lucia can cater to all types of travelers, from backpackers to luxury seekers. Here's a rough idea of daily costs:

- Budget Travelers ($50 - $100 per day): If you're keeping it simple, you can enjoy St. Lucia on a smaller budget. Think hostels, guesthouses, street food, and public buses. You'll still have an amazing time, just without the frills.
- Mid-Range Travelers ($150 - $300 per day): This is the sweet spot for most visitors. You'll be staying in nice hotels or

Airbnb rentals, dining at local restaurants, and maybe enjoying a few guided tours or activities like snorkeling or hiking.
- Luxury Travelers ($400+ per day): If you're ready to splurge, St. Lucia won't disappoint. Stay in all-inclusive resorts or private villas, indulge in fine dining, and book private tours. This is the perfect way to experience the island in style.

Typical Costs You Can Expect:
- Meals: Street food or casual dining costs about $5 - $15 USD per meal, while a nice dinner at a mid-range restaurant might set you back $20 - $40 USD. Fine dining? You're looking at around $50+ USD per person.
- Transportation: Renting a car starts at about $50 USD per day, while taxis can range from $10 - $30 USD for short trips. Local buses are super cheap, usually less than $2 USD per ride.
- Activities: Guided tours (like snorkeling trips or hiking Gros Piton) generally cost between $50 - $150 USD, depending on the length and inclusivity.

Money Tips:
- ATMs are widely available in bigger towns like Castries and Rodney Bay, dispensing local currency.
- Notify your bank before you travel to avoid any issues with your cards.

- Tipping is customary in St. Lucia. Leave 10-15% at restaurants if service isn't included, and tip guides, drivers, and hotel staff as you feel appropriate.

D. Health and Safety Tips

Your trip to St. Lucia should be all about sunshine, relaxation, and adventure. To help keep it that way, let's go over a few health and safety tips so you can enjoy your vacation worry-free. Don't stress—it's mostly common-sense stuff, but it's good to be prepared.

Stay Healthy on the Island
First things first: there are no required vaccines to visit St. Lucia, but it's always a smart move to make sure you're up-to-date on standard shots like hepatitis A, hepatitis B, and typhoid. If you're planning to spend a lot of time outdoors (and why wouldn't you?), it's a good idea to pack insect repellent with DEET to protect against mosquitoes. While malaria isn't a concern here, the island does have some cases of dengue fever, so keep those bites to a minimum.

Tap water in St. Lucia is generally safe to drink, but many travelers prefer to stick with bottled water, especially in more rural areas. It's also a good idea to stay hydrated (the sun is no joke here!) and protect yourself with sunscreen, a hat, and plenty of breaks in the shade.

Emergency Contacts and Health Services
In case of a medical emergency, St. Lucia has several hospitals and clinics, with Victoria Hospital in Castries being the main facility. There are also private clinics like the Tapion Hospital for quicker, more specialized care. It's wise to have travel insurance that covers medical expenses, just in case. Save these emergency numbers on your phone:
- General Emergency: 911
- Police: 999
- Ambulance: 911

If you need a pharmacy, you'll find them in most towns, well-stocked with over-the-counter medications and first-aid supplies.

Safety First: Common Sense Tips
St. Lucia is a friendly and welcoming place, but like anywhere in the world, it's important to be aware of your surroundings. Here are some quick tips to keep you safe:
- Avoid carrying large amounts of cash or flashy jewelry. It's best to keep valuables in a hotel safe.
- Stick to well-lit, populated areas, especially at night. While most neighborhoods are safe, it's smart to avoid walking alone in unfamiliar places after dark.

- Watch your belongings at the beach. Use a waterproof pouch for your phone and wallet, and don't leave your things unattended while you swim.

Ocean Safety
The beaches in St. Lucia are gorgeous, but the waves can be stronger than they look, especially on the Atlantic side of the island. Pay attention to local flags and warnings about swimming conditions. If you're planning on snorkeling or diving, go with a reputable tour operator for the safest experience.

Driving Tips
If you're renting a car, remember that St. Lucia drives on the left side of the road (thanks to its British influence). The roads can be narrow and winding, especially in the hills, so take it slow and watch out for sharp turns. It's also good to know that local drivers can be a bit aggressive, so keep your eyes on the road and be ready to react.

Local Wildlife and Nature Tips
St. Lucia's nature is one of its biggest draws, but remember—you're sharing the island with some amazing wildlife. While hiking, keep an eye out for snakes (like the non-venomous boa constrictor) and avoid touching any unfamiliar plants. If you're heading to the Sulphur Springs for a mud bath, follow the safety guidelines to avoid burns from the hot springs.

E. Language and Local Etiquette

One of the best ways to connect with the locals is by learning a bit about the island's language and culture. Trust me, a little effort goes a long way here, and you'll find the people of St. Lucia to be incredibly friendly and welcoming.

Language Basics
St. Lucia's official language is English, so you won't have any trouble communicating. However, you'll also hear Kwéyòl (Creole) spoken by locals. It's a French-based Creole language that's woven into the daily life and culture of the island. Even if you don't speak Kwéyòl, learning a few simple phrases can bring a smile to anyone's face:

1. Basic Greetings

1. Bonjou! (Good morning!)
   Use: To greet someone in the morning.
   Pronunciation: bon-ZHOO

2. Bonswa! (Good evening!)
   Use: To greet someone in the evening.
   Pronunciation: bon-SWAH

3. Kouman ou yé? (How are you?)
   Use: To ask someone how they are doing.
   Pronunciation: KOO-man oo YAY

4. Mesi! (Thank you!)
Use: To express gratitude.
Pronunciation: meh-SEE

5. Pa ni pwoblem. (No problem.)
Use: To say "It's okay" or "No worries."
Pronunciation: pah NEE PROB-lem

2. Asking for Help

6. Ki koté mwen pé jwenn...? (Where can I find...?)
Use: To ask for directions or the location of something.
Pronunciation: kee KOH-teh mweh peh ZHEN

7. Ou pé édé mwen, silvouplé? (Can you help me, please?)
Use: When you need assistance.
Pronunciation: oo PEH eh-DEH mweh, SEEL-voo-PLAY

8. Mwen pèdi. (I am lost.)
Use: To let someone know you need help finding your way.
Pronunciation: mweh PEH-dee

3. Shopping and Dining

9. Konbyen sa koute? (How much does this cost?)
Use: To ask for the price of an item.
Pronunciation: KON-byen sah koo-TEH

10. Mwen vlé sa, silvouplé. (I would like this, please.)
   Use: When ordering food or purchasing something.
   Pronunciation: mweh VLAY sah, SEEL-voo-PLAY

11. Èske sa bon? (Is this good?)
   Use: To ask if a dish or item is recommended.
   Pronunciation: ESS-keh sah BAWN

12. Koté twalet la? (Where is the bathroom?)
   Use: To ask for the location of the restroom.
   Pronunciation: koh-TEH twa-LET lah

4. Socializing

13. Mwen kontan wè ou! (I'm happy to see you!)
   Use: When meeting someone you know or greeting a local.
   Pronunciation: mweh KON-tan weh oo

14. Nou ka fè fèt! (Let's celebrate!)
   Use: To suggest having fun or celebrating together.
   Pronunciation: noo kah FEH fet

5. Goodbyes and Well Wishes

15. Orevwa! (Goodbye!)
   Use: To say farewell.
   Pronunciation: OH-reh-vwah

Don't worry if you're not fluent—locals appreciate the effort and will often respond warmly.

Greetings and Politeness
In St. Lucia, it's common courtesy to greet people with a friendly "Good morning" or "Good afternoon," even if you're just passing by. Islanders value politeness, so start your interactions with a smile and a greeting before diving into questions or requests. If you're in a market or small shop, a quick "Bonjou" can go a long way in breaking the ice.

Respect for the Island's Culture
St. Lucians are proud of their diverse heritage, which is a blend of African, French, and British influences. You'll notice this mix in the local music, dance, festivals, and food. If you get a chance, join in on a street party in Gros Islet or a cultural festival like Jounen Kwéyòl (Creole Day). It's the best way to experience the vibrant spirit of the island.

Dress Code and Behavior
While St. Lucia has a laid-back, tropical vibe, locals tend to dress modestly, especially in towns and villages. It's totally fine to rock your swimsuit at the beach, but when you're heading into shops, restaurants, or local areas, it's respectful to cover up a bit with a t-shirt and shorts. Topless sunbathing is a no-go on public beaches,

so keep that in mind if you're looking to sunbathe.

When it comes to behavior, St. Lucians are warm and welcoming, but they value respect. Be mindful of taking photos of people without asking first, especially in more rural areas or during cultural events. A simple "May I?" goes a long way.

Tipping Etiquette
Tipping isn't mandatory in St. Lucia, but it's always appreciated for good service. In restaurants, it's customary to leave a 10-15% tip if service isn't already included. For taxi drivers, tour guides, and hotel staff, tipping is a kind gesture that will always be met with gratitude.

A Few Local Customs
- Don't be in a rush. Island time is a real thing here, and life moves at a slower, more relaxed pace. Be patient and embrace the laid-back lifestyle.
- Join the conversation. St. Lucians love to chat, and if you're open to it, you might end up in some wonderful conversations with locals. It's a great way to learn about the island's culture and pick up insider tips on where to go and what to see.

36

Chapter 3: Getting to and Around St. Lucia

A. Flights and Arrival: Airports Overview

St. Lucia is served by two main airports: Hewanorra International Airport (UVF) and George F.L. Charles Airport (SLU). Let's explore each to help you choose the best arrival point for your adventure.

1. Hewanorra International Airport (UVF)

Hewanorra International Airport (UVF)

Hewanorra International Airport
Vieux Fort, St Lucia
3.7 ★★★★
View larger map

Directions

SCAN THE QR CODE

1. Open your device camera app.
2. Position the QR code in the camera frame.
3. Hold your phone steady.
4. Wait for the code to be recognized.
5. Once recognized, tap on the notification or follow the prompt to access the content or action associated with the Qr code

Location: Situated near Vieux Fort on the southern tip of the island, approximately 53.4 km (33.2 miles) from the capital city, Castries.

History: Originally established as Beane Army Airfield during World War II, it was later transformed into a commercial airport and renamed Hewanorra International Airport.

Contact Information:
- Phone: +1 758-454-6355
- Website: [Saint Lucia Air and Sea Ports Authority](www.slaspa.com)

Access: Accessible via the main highway connecting Vieux Fort to Castries. Taxis and car rental services are readily available at the airport.

Facilities: As the larger of St. Lucia's two airports, UVF handles most international flights, accommodating aircraft such as Boeing 747s and Airbus A330s. The airport offers amenities including dining options, duty-free shopping, and car rental services.

Airlines and Destinations: UVF serves as the primary gateway for international travelers, with direct flights from major cities in the U.S., Canada, and Europe. Airlines such as American Airlines, Delta, JetBlue, Air Canada, British Airways, and Virgin Atlantic operate here.

Transportation to Resorts: Many resorts offer shuttle services from UVF. For instance, Sandals Resorts provide transfers to their properties, with travel times ranging from approximately 1 hour and 10 minutes to 1 hour and 40 minutes, depending on the resort's location.

2. George F.L. Charles Airport (SLU)

George F. L. Charles Airport
St Lucia

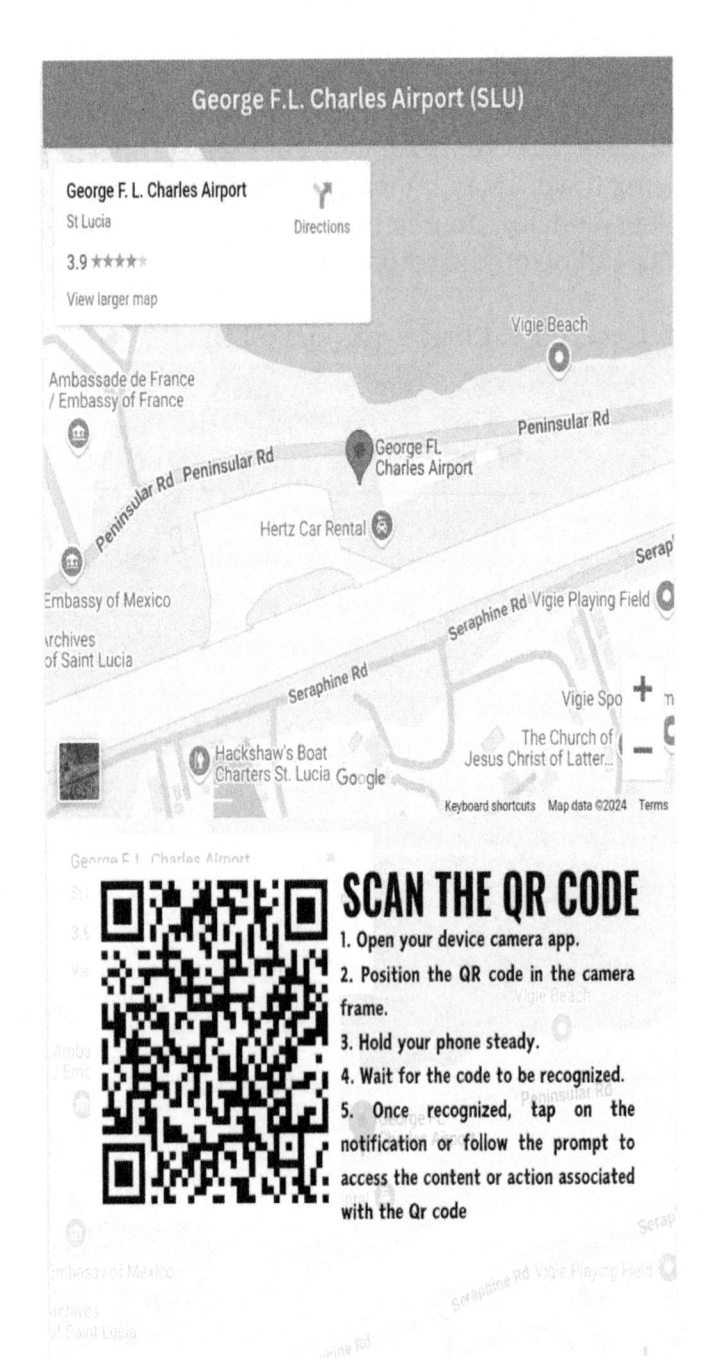

3.9 ★★★★

View larger map

SCAN THE QR CODE

1. Open your device camera app.
2. Position the QR code in the camera frame.
3. Hold your phone steady.
4. Wait for the code to be recognized.
5. Once recognized, tap on the notification or follow the prompt to access the content or action associated with the Qr code

Location: Located in Castries, the capital city, on the northwest coast of St. Lucia.

History: Formerly known as Vigie Airport, it was renamed in honor of George F.L. Charles, a prominent St. Lucian politician.

Contact Information:
- Phone: +1 758-452-2596
- Website: [Saint Lucia Air and Sea Ports Authority](www.slaspa.com/)

Access: Conveniently situated just minutes from downtown Castries, making it easily accessible by taxi or local transportation.

Facilities: SLU is a smaller airport primarily handling regional flights within the Caribbean. Facilities include a few shops, a snack bar, and car rental services.

Airlines and Destinations: SLU caters to inter-island travel, with airlines like LIAT and Caribbean Airlines offering flights to neighboring islands such as Barbados, Antigua, and Trinidad.

Transportation to Resorts: Due to its central location, SLU is closer to many northern resorts. For example, Sandals Halcyon Beach is approximately a 5-minute drive from SLU, making it a convenient option for travelers arriving from other Caribbean destinations.

Choosing the Right Airport

- International Travelers: If you're flying from North America or Europe, Hewanorra International Airport (UVF) is your primary entry point. While it's farther from northern resorts, the scenic drive offers a glimpse of the island's beauty.

- Regional Travelers: For those coming from neighboring Caribbean islands, George F.L. Charles Airport (SLU) provides a more convenient arrival point, especially if your accommodations are in the northern part of the island.

Booking Flights

- International Flights: Major airlines offer direct flights to UVF. It's advisable to book well in advance, especially during peak travel seasons, to secure the best fares and preferred travel dates.

- Regional Flights: For inter-island travel, airlines like LIAT and Caribbean Airlines operate flights to SLU. Check their official websites or consult with a travel agent for schedules and bookings.

Arrival Tips

- Customs and Immigration: Upon arrival, you'll go through customs and immigration. Ensure you have all necessary documents, including a valid passport and return ticket.

- Transportation: Pre-arranging airport transfers with your hotel or resort can provide a seamless transition from the airport to your accommodation. Alternatively, taxis are available at both airports, with fares varying based on distance.

- Currency Exchange: While the Eastern Caribbean Dollar (XCD) is the official currency, U.S. dollars are widely accepted. Currency exchange services are available at the airports, but rates may be more favorable at local banks or ATMs.

B. Transportation Options: Taxis, Buses, and Car Rentals

Alright, you've landed in St. Lucia—now it's time to get moving! The island may be small, but there are plenty of ways to explore its beauty. Here's a rundown of your main transportation options and what you need to know to get around like a pro.

Taxis

Taxis are one of the most popular ways to get around St. Lucia, especially if you want a simple, no-fuss option. Taxis here aren't metered, so it's best to agree on a fare before you start your ride. The good news is that most taxi drivers are friendly and knowledgeable—they double as tour guides, sharing stories and tips about the best local spots.

- Where to Find Taxis: You can easily find taxis at the airports, hotels, and major tourist areas like Rodney Bay and Soufrière. Look for cars with the "TX" license plate prefix.
- Cost: A ride from Hewanorra International Airport (UVF) to Castries or the popular resort areas in the north costs around $75 - $100 USD. Shorter trips, like from Castries to Marigot Bay, range from $20 - $30 USD.
- Pro Tip: If you're up for it, ask your driver about custom tours—many will take you on a personalized island adventure, showing you hidden gems and local favorites.

Local Buses

If you want to experience St. Lucia like a local (and save some money), hop on a local bus. These minibuses are a fun and affordable way to get around, and they're a great option if you don't mind a bit of a bumpy ride and a lively atmosphere.

- Where to Catch the Bus: Bus stops are marked along major roads, and you can flag one down pretty much anywhere. In Castries, head to the Derek Walcott Square bus terminal, where you'll find buses heading to various parts of the island.
- Cost: A typical bus fare is around $1 - $3 USD, depending on the distance. It's incredibly budget-friendly, but be prepared for crowded rides, especially during rush hours.
- Pro Tip: Buses don't follow strict schedules—they leave when they're full. It's part of the island's laid-back vibe, so just go with the flow!

Car Rentals

Renting a car is a fantastic choice if you prefer the freedom to explore the island on your own schedule. St. Lucia's roads can be narrow and winding, especially in the hills, but the scenic drives are well worth it. Just remember: in St. Lucia, you drive on the left side of the road!

- Where to Rent: Car rental agencies are located at both Hewanorra International Airport (UVF) and George F.L. Charles Airport (SLU), as well as in major tourist

hubs like Rodney Bay. Popular companies include Hertz, Avis, and Drive-a-Matic.
- Cost: Expect to pay around $50 - $100 USD per day, depending on the type of vehicle and the season. 4x4 vehicles are a great choice if you plan to explore off-the-beaten-path spots or rugged terrain.
- What You Need: You'll need a valid driver's license and may need to purchase a temporary St. Lucian driving permit, which costs about $20 USD. Most rental agencies can issue this permit on the spot.
- Pro Tip: Gas stations are not self-service, so just pull up and let the attendant know how much fuel you need. Keep some cash handy, as not all gas stations accept credit cards.

Private Transfers and Shuttles

For those looking for a bit more comfort and convenience, private transfers and shuttle services are a great option. Many resorts offer pre-arranged transfers from the airport, so you can relax and enjoy the scenic ride without worrying about navigation. It's a great way to kick off your vacation, especially if you're arriving after a long flight.
- How to Book: You can arrange private transfers through your hotel or book

online via services like Island Routes and St. Lucia Airport Shuttle. Prices range from $80 - $150 USD for a one-way trip, depending on the distance.
- Pro Tip: For a memorable start to your vacation, opt for a luxury transfer, complete with cold towels, snacks, and a rum punch welcome drink. It's a great way to start your St. Lucian adventure in style!

Scooter and Bike Rentals

Feeling adventurous? Consider renting a scooter or bicycle to explore at your own pace. It's a fun way to navigate the smaller roads and trails, especially if you're staying in areas like Soufrière or Marigot Bay.

- Cost: Scooter rentals typically start at $30 - $50 USD per day, while bicycles go for around $15 - $25 USD per day.
- Safety Tip: Always wear a helmet (it's the law here), and be cautious on the winding roads, especially if you're new to driving on the left side.

C. Island Hopping and Day Trips

Ready to explore beyond the main island? St. Lucia is the perfect base for hopping to nearby islands and enjoying some incredible day trips. The island's central location in the Caribbean makes it easy to explore the neighboring gems of the Windward Islands, whether you're looking for secluded beaches, vibrant coral reefs, or a taste of local culture in nearby communities.

Island Hopping

St. Lucia is surrounded by a chain of stunning islands, each offering its own unique vibe and experiences. Here's a look at some popular nearby destinations and how to get there:

1. Martinique:

Just a short 90-minute ferry ride from St. Lucia, Martinique feels like a slice of France in the Caribbean. The island is known for its French-inspired cuisine, rum distilleries, and beautiful beaches. If you're a foodie, you'll love exploring the bakeries and sampling local dishes like Accras de Morue (saltfish fritters).

- How to Get There: Take the Express des Îles ferry from Castries Harbor. Tickets range from $90 to $130 USD round trip.
- Pro Tip: Bring your passport, as you'll be entering a French territory, and don't miss the chance to visit the vibrant market in Fort-de-France.

2. The Grenadines:

For a true island-hopping adventure, consider a day trip to the Grenadines, a collection of small islands south of St. Lucia. This area is famous for its sailing trips, crystal-clear waters, and vibrant

marine life. It's a dream spot for snorkeling and diving.
- How to Get There: Book a guided sailing tour or catamaran excursion, typically costing $150 - $250 USD per person, including lunch and snorkeling gear.
- Pro Tip: Visit the uninhabited island of Tobago Cays for an unforgettable snorkeling experience with sea turtles.

3. St. Vincent: The Land of Volcanoes

If you're up for an adventure, head over to St. Vincent, known for its volcanic landscapes and black sand beaches. Hike up La Soufrière, an active volcano, for breathtaking views of the island and the surrounding sea.
- How to Get There: Take a short 45-minute flight from George F.L. Charles Airport (SLU) or book a private speedboat tour.
- Pro Tip: Bring sturdy hiking shoes for the volcano trek and plenty of water—the climb can be challenging but is well worth it!

Top Day Trips in St. Lucia

If you'd rather stay on the island but still want to explore beyond your resort, there are plenty of day trips that offer a taste of St. Lucia's natural beauty and culture.

1. Soufrière and the Pitons:

Soufrière is the heart of St. Lucia's volcanic landscape and home to the iconic Pitons, a UNESCO World Heritage Site. Spend the day visiting the Sulphur Springs—the world's only drive-in volcano—where you can take a mud bath and soak in the mineral-rich waters.

- How to Get There: Book a guided tour from Castries or Rodney Bay, or rent a car and drive (about 1.5 hours from the north).
- Cost: Entry to the Sulphur Springs is around $10 USD per person, and a guided tour of the Pitons costs about $50 - $100 USD.
- Pro Tip: Visit early in the morning to beat the crowds and enjoy cooler temperatures for hiking.

2. Pigeon Island National Park:

For a mix of history and beach time, head to Pigeon Island National Park. It's a beautiful spot with historic ruins, hiking trails, and two stunning beaches. You can explore the remnants of old military forts and learn about the island's past while taking in spectacular views of the Caribbean Sea.

- How to Get There: Pigeon Island is located in the north, near Rodney Bay. It's a quick 10-minute drive from most northern resorts.
- Cost: The entrance fee is about $8 USD per person.

52

Chapter 4: Accommodations for Every Budget

A. Top Luxury Resorts

Ready to dive into paradise? Let's check out the top luxury resorts that will make your stay unforgettable.

1. Jade Mountain Resort

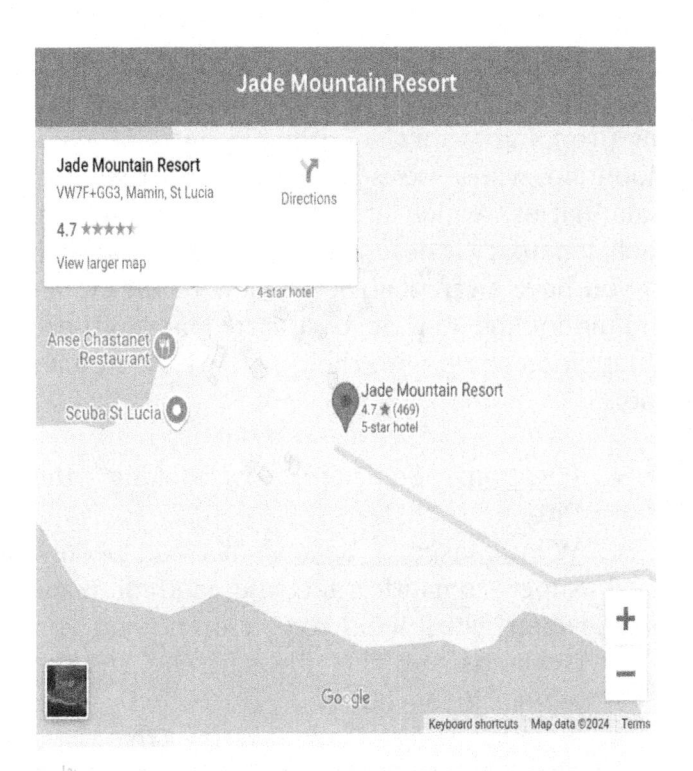

Jade Mountain Resort

Jade Mountain Resort
VW7F+GG3, Mamin, St Lucia
4.7 ★★★★★
View larger map

Jade Mountain Resort
4.7 ★ (469)
5-star hotel

SCAN THE QR CODE

1. Open your device camera app.
2. Position the QR code in the camera frame.
3. Hold your phone steady.
4. Wait for the code to be recognized.
5. Once recognized, tap on the notification or follow the prompt to access the content or action associated with the Qr code

This is the place you've seen in travel magazines—the one with the open-air rooms and jaw-dropping views of the Pitons. At Jade Mountain, you'll be staying in what they call "sanctuaries," which are more than just rooms. Each sanctuary is designed without a fourth wall, so you have an unobstructed view of the ocean and mountains. And the best part? Many of these sanctuaries come with their own private infinity pool.

- Location: Soufrière, overlooking the Pitons
- What Makes It Special: It's adults-only, super romantic, and the kind of place where you'll feel like you're on your own private island. The vibe is serene, and the service is top-notch.
- Dining: You've got to try the Jade Mountain Club restaurant—it's all about fresh, organic ingredients grown right on the resort's farm.
- Activities: From yoga sessions to snorkeling tours, they've got everything covered. And if you're feeling adventurous, take a guided hike up the Pitons.
- Rates: Starting at around $1,200 per night (but trust me, it's worth it).
- Contact: [www.jademountain.com] | +1 758-459-4000

Pro Tip: If you're celebrating something special, let them know—they often surprise guests with champagne and treats.

2. Sugar Beach, A Viceroy Resort

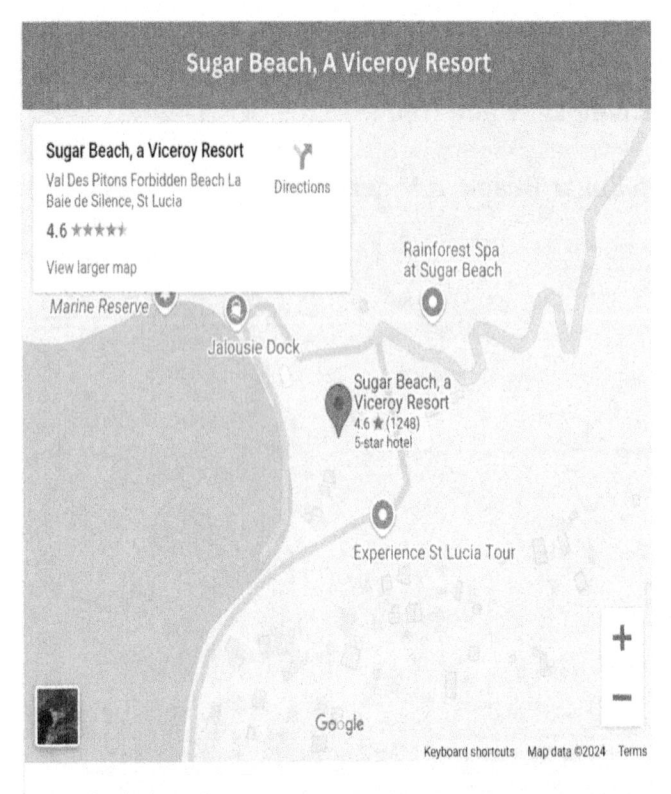

Sugar Beach, A Viceroy Resort

Sugar Beach, a Viceroy Resort
Val Des Pitons Forbidden Beach La Baie de Silence, St Lucia
4.6 ★★★★⯪
View larger map

Directions

Rainforest Spa at Sugar Beach

Marine Reserve

Jalousie Dock

Sugar Beach, a Viceroy Resort
4.6 ★ (1248)
5-star hotel

Experience St Lucia Tour

Google

Keyboard shortcuts   Map data ©2024   Terms

SCAN THE QR CODE

1. Open your device camera app.
2. Position the QR code in the camera frame.
3. Hold your phone steady.
4. Wait for the code to be recognized.
5. Once recognized, tap on the notification or follow the prompt to access the content or action associated with the Qr code

If lounging on a white sand beach between the Pitons sounds like your kind of paradise, then Sugar Beach is calling your name. This resort was once a working sugar plantation, so it blends history with modern luxury. Imagine private beachfront villas, your own butler, and direct access to one of the best snorkeling spots on the island.

- Location: Right between Gros Piton and Petit Piton, near Soufrière
- Why You'll Love It: Private plunge pools, personalized service, and that dreamy beach vibe. It's perfect for honeymooners and couples.
- Dining: The Cane Bar is a must-visit if you love rum—try a rum tasting session! For dining, The Terrace offers delicious seafood dishes with a view of the Pitons.
- Spa: The Rainforest Spa feels like a hidden sanctuary, with treatments in treehouse-style rooms. It's the ultimate relaxation experience.
- Rates: From $900 to $2,500 per night, depending on the season and room type.
- Contact: www.viceroyhotelsandresorts.com/sugar-beach | +1 758-456-8000

Pro Tip: Book a sunset cruise—you'll get incredible views of the Pitons while enjoying champagne and snacks.

3. Ladera Resort

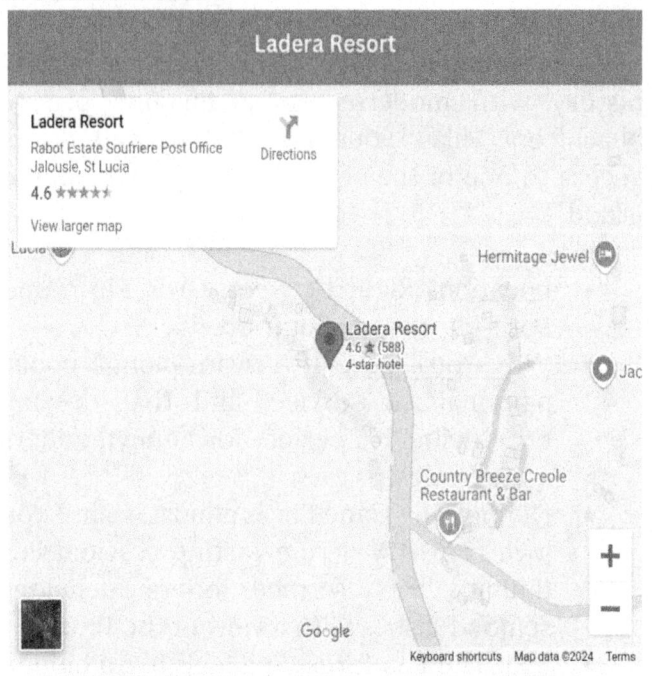

Ladera Resort
Rabot Estate Soufriere Post Office
Jalousie, St Lucia
4.6 ★★★★★
View larger map

Directions

Ladera Resort
4.6 ★ (588)
4-star hotel

SCAN THE QR CODE
1. Open your device camera app.
2. Position the QR code in the camera frame.
3. Hold your phone steady.
4. Wait for the code to be recognized.
5. Once recognized, tap on the notification or follow the prompt to access the content or action associated with the Qr code

Imagine waking up to the sound of birds, the fresh Caribbean breeze, and views of the Pitons from your bed. At Ladera Resort, every room has an open wall facing the mountains, making you feel like you're living in a luxury treehouse. It's an adults-only resort, perfect for couples looking to escape and reconnect with nature.

- Location: High above Soufrière, offering panoramic views of the Pitons
- What's Unique: Each suite comes with its own plunge pool, and the design uses local materials like volcanic stone and tropical hardwoods.
- Dining: Dasheene is the on-site restaurant, famous for its fresh, locally-sourced dishes. Try the Caribbean jerk chicken—it's a guest favorite!
- Activities: They offer guided hikes, cooking classes, and tours of the local cocoa plantations (chocolate lovers, this one's for you).
- Rates: Prices start at $800 per night.
- Contact: [www.ladera.com]| +1 758-459-6600

Pro Tip: Go for a sunrise yoga session—it's the perfect way to start your day with a view you'll never forget.

4. Sandals Grande St. Lucian

Looking for an all-inclusive resort where you don't have to worry about anything? Sandals Grande St. Lucian is all about indulgence. Picture over-the-water bungalows, swim-up bars, and endless activities—all included in your stay. It's great for couples who want a mix of relaxation and adventure.

- Location: On its own private peninsula in Rodney Bay
- Highlights: Swim-up suites, a mile-long beach, and access to two other Sandals resorts on the island (more dining and activity options!).
- Dining: With 12 restaurants, you can have a different cuisine every night—Italian, French, Japanese, you name it.
- Activities: Unlimited scuba diving, snorkeling, paddleboarding, and nightly beach parties. It's impossible to get bored here.
- Rates: All-inclusive packages start at $700 per night.
- Contact: [www.sandals.com] | +1 888-SANDALS

Pro Tip: Book an over-the-water bungalow for a truly unforgettable experience. You'll have a glass floor in your room to watch the fish swimming below!

5. Cap Maison

If you prefer boutique-style luxury, Cap Maison is your spot. Perched on a cliff, it offers breathtaking ocean views, Spanish-inspired architecture, and a vibe that's both elegant and laid-back. It's perfect for travelers who want a more intimate and private experience.

- Location: Smugglers Cove, near Gros Islet
- What to Expect: Spacious suites, a private beach, and one of the best rooftop restaurants on the island—The Cliff at Cap.
- Activities: They offer everything from sailing trips and snorkeling to wine tastings in their own cellar.
- Rates: Starting at $600 per night.
- Contact: [www.capmaison.com] | +1 758-457-8670

Pro Tip: Book a private dinner on the beach for a romantic experience you'll remember forever.

B. Mid-Range Hotels and Boutique Stays

1. Bay Gardens Beach Resort & Spa

SCAN THE QR CODE

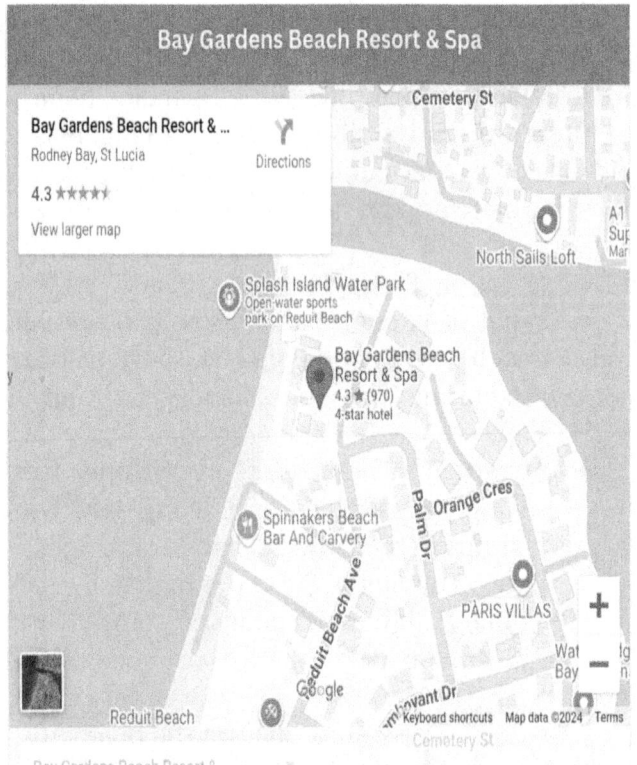

1. Open your device camera app.
2. Position the QR code in the camera frame.
3. Hold your phone steady.
4. Wait for the code to be recognized.
5. Once recognized, tap on the notification or follow the prompt to access the content or action associated with the Qr code

If you're looking for a lively atmosphere with lots of activities, Bay Gardens Beach Resort is a fantastic choice. Located right on the popular Reduit Beach, this resort has everything you need for a relaxing and fun vacation, including a great location near shops, restaurants, and bars.

- <u>Location</u>: Rodney Bay, in the heart of St. Lucia's main tourist area
- <u>What You'll Love:</u> The beachfront location, spacious rooms, and family-friendly vibe. They also have a water park—perfect if you're traveling with kids!
- <u>Dining:</u> On-site restaurants like Hi Tide offer delicious Caribbean dishes, and the pool bar serves up refreshing cocktails.
- <u>Activities</u>: Enjoy water sports, spa treatments, and free shuttle services to the Bay Gardens Hotel, where you can use additional amenities like the spa and gym.
- <u>Rates:</u> Rooms start at $200 - $350 per night, depending on the season.
- <u>Contact</u>: [www.baygardensresorts.com] | +1 758-457-8000

<u>Pro Tip:</u> Book directly through their website to take advantage of special packages that include free breakfast or spa credits.

2. The Ginger Lily Hotel

The Ginger Lily Hotel

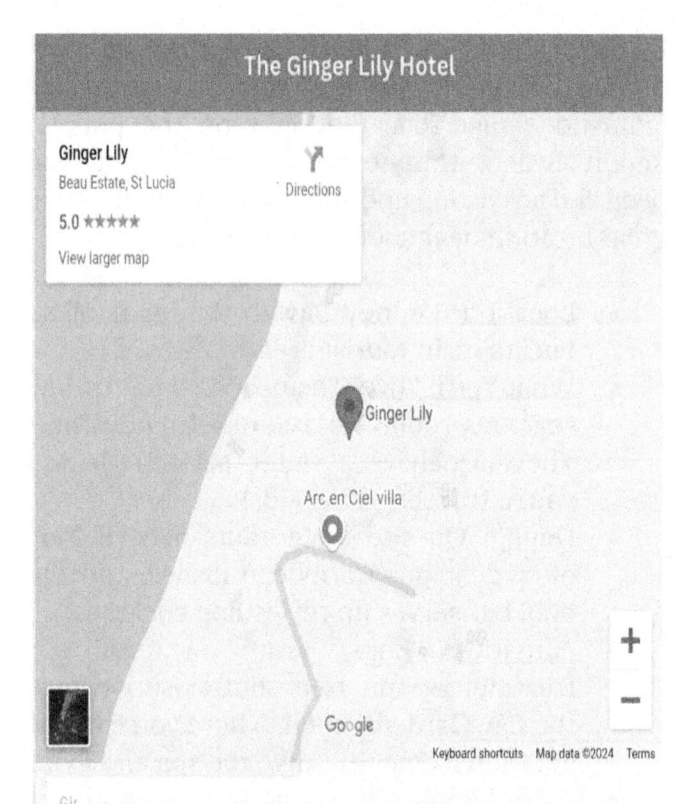

Ginger Lily
Beau Estate, St Lucia
5.0 ★★★★★
View larger map

Directions

Ginger Lily
Arc en Ciel villa

Google
Keyboard shortcuts Map data ©2024 Terms

SCAN THE QR CODE

1. Open your device camera app.
2. Position the QR code in the camera frame.
3. Hold your phone steady.
4. Wait for the code to be recognized.
5. Once recognized, tap on the notification or follow the prompt to access the content or action associated with the Qr code

If you're after a quieter, more intimate experience, The Ginger Lily Hotel in Rodney Bay is a lovely boutique option. It's a small property with just 11 rooms, so you'll feel like you have your own little slice of paradise. The staff is incredibly friendly, and the hotel's cozy vibe makes it perfect for couples or solo travelers looking for a peaceful escape.

- Location: Just a short walk from Reduit Beach and the bustling shops of Rodney Bay
- What Makes It Special: The rooms are spacious, with bright, tropical décor and private balconies. It's a peaceful retreat with a personal touch.
- Dining: While there's no on-site restaurant, you're only steps away from local dining options. The staff can recommend great spots nearby.
- Rates: Starting at $150 - $250 per night, making it a great value for the area.
- Contact: [www.gingerlilyhotel.com] | +1 758-452-8756

Pro Tip: Ask the front desk for tips on the best local eateries—you'll find some hidden gems just around the corner.

3. Fond Doux Eco Resort

Looking for something a bit more unique? Fond Doux Eco Resort offers a stay unlike any other.

This charming eco-friendly resort is set on a 250-year-old working cocoa plantation, surrounded by lush rainforest. It's a great option if you want to feel close to nature while enjoying all the comforts of a mid-range stay.

- Location: Soufrière, nestled in the rainforest, close to the Pitons and Sulphur Springs
- Why You'll Love It: The cottages are rustic yet comfortable, with lots of privacy. You'll wake up to the sounds of birds and the scent of fresh cocoa.
- Dining: Enjoy farm-to-table dining at Bamboo Restaurant, where the ingredients are sourced directly from the plantation. Try the fresh cocoa tea—it's a must!
- Activities: They offer cocoa plantation tours, hiking trails, and yoga classes. Plus, it's just a short drive to attractions like the Tet Paul Nature Trail.
- Rates: Rooms range from $180 - $300 per night, depending on the cottage type.
- Contact: [www.fonddouxresort.com] | +1 758-459-7545

Pro Tip: Book a plantation tour for a behind-the-scenes look at how chocolate is made—it's both educational and delicious!

4. The Harbor Club, Curio Collection by Hilton

If you want a bit of style and sophistication without the luxury price tag, check out The Harbor Club. This sleek, modern hotel in Rodney Bay is part of Hilton's Curio Collection, offering all the perks you'd expect from a top hotel, but at mid-range rates.

- Location: Right on the waterfront in Rodney Bay Marina, perfect for exploring the area
- What Stands Out: The stylish design, rooftop pool, and a wide range of dining options make this a great pick for couples or groups of friends.
- Dining: With five on-site restaurants, including the popular Dockside Pizzeria and 14° North, you won't need to leave the hotel for great food.
- Activities: Enjoy the fitness center, spa, and easy access to yacht charters and water sports. They also have live music and entertainment on weekends.
- Rates: Rooms start at $220 - $400 per night, depending on the season and view.
- Contact: [www.theharborclub.com] | +1 758-731-2900

Pro Tip: Head up to the Rooftop Lounge for sunset cocktails—it's one of the best spots to watch the sun go down over the marina.

5. Coco Palm Resort

For those who want a touch of elegance on a budget, Coco Palm Resort is a fantastic option. It's got the look and feel of a high-end boutique hotel, but without the hefty price tag. Located in the heart of Rodney Bay Village, it's close to everything you need—beaches, shops, and nightlife.

- Location: Rodney Bay Village, within walking distance to Reduit Beach
- Why You'll Love It: The friendly staff and cozy rooms make it feel like a home away from home. Plus, the lagoon-style pool is perfect for cooling off after a day of exploring.
- Dining: The on-site restaurant, Ti Bananne Caribbean Bistro, serves delicious Creole and Caribbean dishes. Their Sunday brunch is a local favorite.
- Rates: Rooms start at around $150 per night, making it a great deal for the area.
- Contact: [www.coco-resorts.com] | +1 758-456-2800

Pro Tip: Book a poolside room for direct access to the water—it's like having your own private oasis.

C. Budget-Friendly Options and Hostels

1. The Still Beach House

The Still Beach House

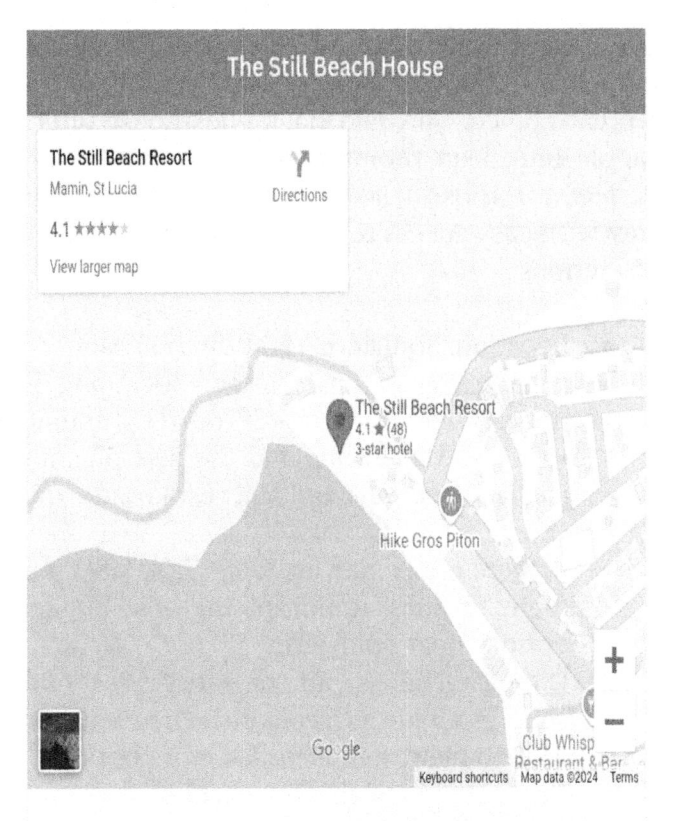

The Still Beach Resort
Mamin, St Lucia

4.1 ★★★★

View larger map

Directions

The Still Beach Resort
4.1 ★ (48)
3-star hotel

Hike Gros Piton

Club Whisp
Restaurant & Bar

Google

Keyboard shortcuts Map data ©2024 Terms

SCAN THE QR CODE

1. Open your device camera app.
2. Position the QR code in the camera frame.
3. Hold your phone steady.
4. Wait for the code to be recognized.
5. Once recognized, tap on the notification or follow the prompt to access the content or action associated with the Qr code

If you want to wake up with your toes practically in the sand, The Still Beach House in Soufrière is a great choice. This laid-back guesthouse offers simple but clean rooms right on the beach. It's perfect for those who want a relaxed, no-frills stay with easy access to the water and the town's attractions.

- Location: Soufrière, right on the beach
- What You'll Love: The location is unbeatable for the price. You get stunning views of the Pitons and the sea, plus it's just a short walk to local restaurants and shops.
- Rates: Rooms start at $70 - $100 USD per night, making it one of the best budget options near Soufrière.
- Dining: There's an on-site restaurant serving up local Creole dishes, or you can walk to nearby eateries for more options.
- Contact: [www.thestillbeachhouse.com] | +1 758-459-5648

Pro Tip: Ask for a room with a balcony so you can enjoy your morning coffee with a view of the Pitons.

2. Charlery's Inn

Charlery's Inn

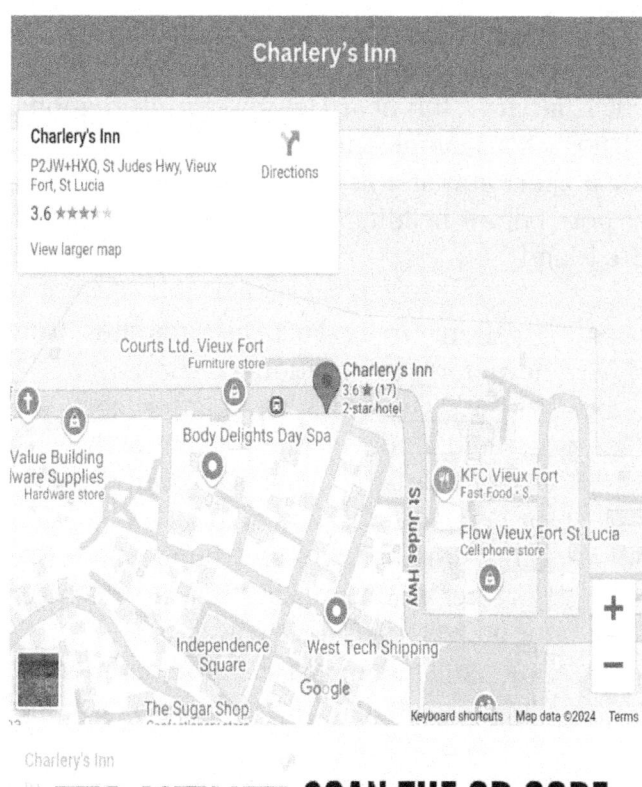

Charlery's Inn
P2JW+HXQ, St Judes Hwy, Vieux Fort, St Lucia

Directions

3.6 ★★★★

View larger map

SCAN THE QR CODE

1. Open your device camera app.
2. Position the QR code in the camera frame.
3. Hold your phone steady.
4. Wait for the code to be recognized.
5. Once recognized, tap on the notification or follow the prompt to access the content or action associated with the Qr code

If you're looking for a convenient and affordable place to crash right after your flight lands, check out Charlery's Inn near Hewanorra International Airport. It's a simple, no-fuss hotel that's perfect for a short stay if you need a place close to the airport before heading off to explore the rest of the island.

- Location: Vieux Fort, just minutes from Hewanorra International Airport
- Why It's Great: It's clean, affordable, and incredibly convenient for late arrivals or early departures. Plus, the staff is known for being friendly and helpful.
- Rates: Rooms start at around $60 - $80 USD per night, making it a great choice for budget-conscious travelers.
- Amenities: Free Wi-Fi, air conditioning, and a small café serving breakfast and snacks.
- Contact: [www.charlerysinn.com] | +1 758-454-6037

Pro Tip: If you have a long layover, this is a great spot to freshen up and grab a quick nap before your next flight.

3. Casa del Vega

Casa del Vega

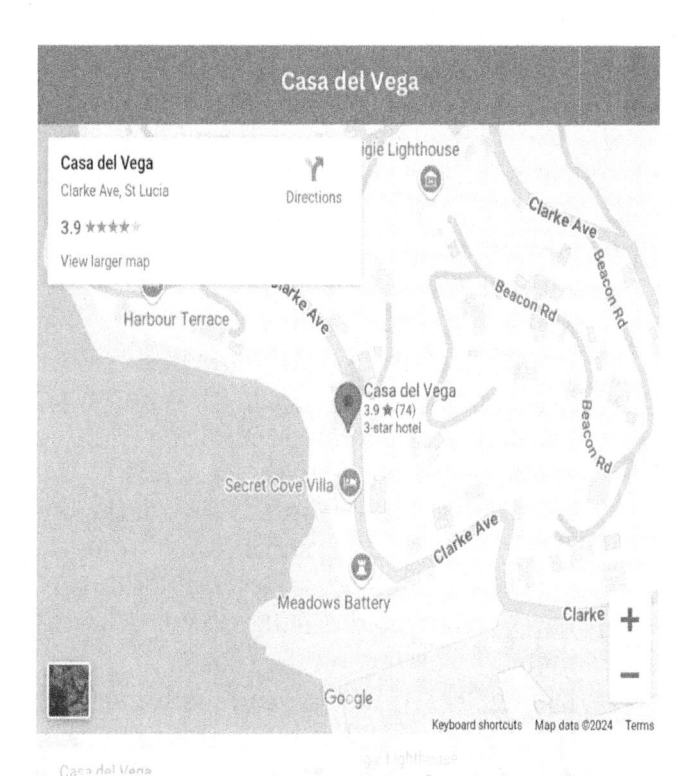

Casa del Vega
Clarke Ave, St Lucia
3.9 ★★★★
View larger map

Directions

SCAN THE QR CODE

1. Open your device camera app.
2. Position the QR code in the camera frame.
3. Hold your phone steady.
4. Wait for the code to be recognized.
5. Once recognized, tap on the notification or follow the prompt to access the content or action associated with the Qr code

For a cozy, home-like stay, Casa del Vega in Castries is a fantastic option. It's a family-run guesthouse that offers warm hospitality and a relaxed atmosphere. Located just a short walk from the capital's main attractions, it's ideal for travelers who want to be in the heart of the action without paying resort prices.

- Location: Castries, near Vigie Beach
- What Makes It Special: The hosts are incredibly welcoming, and it feels like you're staying with friends. The guesthouse has beautiful views of the bay, and you're just a short walk from the beach.
- Rates: Starting at $50 - $90 USD per night, depending on the season.
- Dining: There's no on-site restaurant, but the kitchen facilities allow you to prepare your own meals. Plus, you're close to local markets for fresh ingredients.
- Contact: [www.casadelvega.com] | +1 758-452-4312

Pro Tip: Check out the nearby Vigie Beach for a quiet spot to relax, away from the crowds.

4. Tropical Breeze Guesthouse

If you're a backpacker or solo traveler looking for a sociable, affordable place to stay, head to Tropical Breeze Guesthouse in Gros Islet. It's known for its laid-back vibe and welcoming atmosphere, making it a great place to meet fellow travelers. The guesthouse offers dorm beds and private rooms, so there's something for every budget.

- Location: Gros Islet, near the famous Friday Night Street Party
- What You'll Love: The friendly vibe and the chance to meet other travelers. It's close to the beach and all the action in Gros Islet.
- Rates: Dorm beds start at $20 USD per night, and private rooms are available for $50 - $80 USD.
- Amenities: Free Wi-Fi, shared kitchen facilities, and a common area where guests often hang out and swap travel stories.
- Contact: Phone: +1 758-450-8718

Pro Tip: Stay over a Friday night to experience the Gros Islet Street Party, where you can dance, eat local street food, and have a blast with both locals and tourists.

5. JJ's Paradise Hotel

Tucked away in the lush greenery of Marigot Bay, JJ's Paradise Hotel offers budget-friendly rooms with a touch of local charm. It's a great choice if you want to be close to Marigot Bay's famous waterfront but don't want to pay the premium prices of the nearby resorts.

- Location: Marigot Bay, nestled in the hills
- What Stands Out: The tropical garden setting makes you feel like you're in your own little oasis. It's peaceful and quiet, but just a short walk to the lively marina area.
- Rates: Rooms start at $75 - $120 USD per night, making it an excellent deal for the area.
- Dining: The on-site restaurant serves tasty local dishes, and there's a poolside bar for drinks and snacks.
- Contact: www.jjsparadise.com | +1 758-451-4076

Pro Tip: Take the ferry across Marigot Bay for some of the best views and photo ops of your trip.

78

Chapter 5: Itinerary Planning

A. Sample 3-Day Itinerary

Hey there, adventurer! Only got three days to spend in St. Lucia? No worries—you can still pack in a ton of amazing experiences. Here's the ultimate 3-day itinerary that will leave you craving for more!

Day 1: Beaches, Cocktails, and a Stunning Sunset

Morning: Welcome to St. Lucia!
You've landed in the Caribbean's best-kept secret—welcome! Whether you're flying into Hewanorra International Airport (UVF) or George F.L. Charles Airport (SLU), grab a taxi or your pre-booked transfer and head straight to your hotel. If you're staying in Rodney Bay, you're in

for a treat. Check in, drop your bags, and get ready to kick off your adventure.

Afternoon: Chill at Reduit Beach
It's your first day, so let's ease into it with some serious beach time. Head to Reduit Beach, one of the island's most popular spots. Picture this: soft white sand, crystal-clear water, and plenty of beach bars serving up rum punches. Rent a lounger, dip your toes in the water, and soak up the sun. If you're feeling adventurous, try jet skiing or paddleboarding—there's no better way to enjoy that gorgeous Caribbean Sea.

Evening: Sunset Dinner at Marigot Bay
When the sun starts to dip, head over to Marigot Bay, a spot so beautiful it looks like it's straight out of a postcard. Grab a table at Hurricane Hole Restaurant, order the catch of the day, and watch the sunset paint the sky with shades of pink and orange. It's the perfect end to your first day on the island.

Insider Tip: If you've got energy to spare, hit up the bars in Rodney Bay. It's the nightlife hub of St. Lucia, with live music, dancing, and plenty of fun to be had.

Day 2: The Pitons and Soufrière Adventures

Morning: Explore the Iconic Pitons
Ready for an adventure? Let's head to Soufrière, home to the island's famous twin peaks—Gros

Piton and Petit Piton. If you're up for it, tackle the Gros Piton hike. It's a challenging climb, but trust me, the view from the top is worth every step. Not in the mood for a hike? No problem. Swing by the Sulphur Springs instead, the world's only drive-in volcano. Take a guided tour, then jump into the hot springs for a mineral-rich mud bath. Your skin will thank you!

Afternoon: Lunch and Snorkeling at Anse Chastanet
You've earned a break, so let's head to Anse Chastanet Beach for lunch. Try some local Creole dishes while gazing out at the Pitons—it's a feast for your eyes and your taste buds. Once you're fueled up, grab some snorkeling gear and dive into the turquoise water. The coral reefs here are teeming with colorful fish, and if you're lucky, you might even spot a sea turtle or two.

Evening: Dinner in Soufrière
For dinner, stick around in Soufrière and check out Orlando's Restaurant, a local favorite. The vibe is cozy, and the food? Absolutely mouth-watering. Go for the jerk chicken or fresh grilled fish—you won't be disappointed. After dinner, take a stroll along the waterfront and enjoy the cool evening breeze.

Insider Tip: The Soufrière nightlife is more laid-back, but you might find some live music at a local bar. It's a great way to mingle with locals and experience the island's friendly vibe.

Day 3: Sail, Shop, and Savor Your Last Day

<u>Morning: Sail to Pigeon Island</u>
It's your last day, so let's make it count with a half-day sailing trip to Pigeon Island National Park. This spot is a mix of history, nature, and beaches—all wrapped up in one beautiful package. Explore the old military ruins, hike up to the fort for a panoramic view, or just relax on the beach with a good book. If you're a history buff, you'll love learning about the island's past here.

<u>Afternoon: Lunch and Souvenir Shopping in Castries</u>
Head back to Castries, the capital city, for lunch. Stop at The Coal Pot—a local favorite known for its seafood dishes and waterfront views. After lunch, wander through the Castries Market. It's the perfect place to pick up some last-minute souvenirs like local spices, handmade crafts, and a bottle of St. Lucian rum (trust me, your friends back home will thank you).

<u>Evening: Farewell Dinner at Rodney Bay</u>
For your final night, treat yourself to dinner at Spice of India in Rodney Bay. It's a bit of a twist on local cuisine with an Indian flair, and the flavors are incredible. Order the seafood curry—it's a crowd favorite. Enjoy your meal, sip on a final rum punch, and soak in the island vibes one last time.

Insider Tip: End your night with a walk along the beach under the stars. It's the perfect way to say goodbye to St. Lucia.

Departure Tips:

- Airport Transfer: Give yourself plenty of time for the drive to the airport, especially if you're leaving from Rodney Bay. The trip to Hewanorra International Airport (UVF) takes about 1.5 hours.
- Last-Minute Souvenirs: Grab some locally made chocolate or a St. Lucian spice mix at the airport's duty-free shop. They make great gifts (or treats for yourself!).

B. Sample 5-Day Itinerary

Day 1: Welcome to Paradise—Settle In and Hit the Beach

Morning: Arrival and Check-In
Welcome to St. Lucia! After landing at either Hewanorra International Airport (UVF) or George F.L. Charles Airport (SLU), head straight to your hotel. If you're staying in Rodney Bay or Castries, the drive from UVF will take about 1.5 hours. Settle into your room, drop your bags, and get ready to soak up those island vibes.

Afternoon: Relax at Vigie Beach
Kick off your vacation with a relaxing afternoon at Vigie Beach, a favorite spot for locals. It's close to Castries, making it an easy and breezy first stop. Lay back, sip on a coconut water or rum punch, and let the Caribbean Sea wash away your travel fatigue.

Evening: Sunset Dinner at The Coal Pot
For your first dinner on the island, head to The Coal Pot restaurant by the water. The setting is beautiful, and the seafood is as fresh as it gets. Order the grilled mahi-mahi or the Creole-style shrimp, and pair it with a tropical cocktail. Enjoy the sunset views and let the warm evening breeze welcome you to St. Lucia.

Insider Tip: If you're up for it, take a stroll through the nearby Castries Market before it closes. You'll find local crafts and fresh produce—perfect for a little pre-dinner shopping.

Day 2: Soufrière and the Pitons Adventure

Morning: Hike Gros Piton
Start your day bright and early with a guided hike up Gros Piton. It's one of the island's most iconic landmarks and a must-do for adventurers. The trail is challenging, but your guide will keep you motivated with stories about the island's history and the stunning views at the top will be worth every step.

Afternoon: Lunch at Dasheene and Mud Baths

After your hike, treat yourself to a well-deserved lunch at Dasheene, the restaurant at Ladera Resort. The views of the Pitons are unbeatable, and the food is top-notch. Try the jerk chicken wrap or the seafood platter—it's all delicious! Once you're fueled up, head over to the Sulphur Springs for a rejuvenating mud bath. Slather on the mineral-rich mud, let it dry in the sun, then rinse off in the hot springs. It's nature's spa treatment, and your skin will feel amazing.

Evening: Explore Soufrière and Dinner at Orlando's

Spend your evening exploring the charming town of Soufrière. Walk along the waterfront, visit the local market, and grab dinner at Orlando's Restaurant. It's a cozy spot with a focus on farm-to-table Caribbean cuisine. Order the fresh catch of the day or the spicy lamb curry—you won't be disappointed.

Insider Tip: The local vendors are super friendly, so don't be shy about chatting with them and learning more about the island's culture.

Day 3: Sailing, Snorkeling, and Beach Hopping

Morning: Sail Along the West Coast

Today, we're hitting the water! Book a half-day sailing tour along St. Lucia's stunning west coast. Most tours depart from Rodney Bay or Marigot

Bay and take you past beautiful spots like the Pitons and Anse Chastanet Beach. Bring your camera—the views are Instagram gold!

Afternoon: Snorkeling at Anse Chastanet
Drop anchor at Anse Chastanet for some world-class snorkeling. The reefs here are vibrant and full of life, with colorful fish, corals, and maybe even a sea turtle or two. If you're not into snorkeling, just relax on the beach and soak up the sun.

Evening: Casual Dinner at Marigot Bay
For dinner, head to Marigot Bay and grab a bite at Doolittle's Restaurant. It's a fun, laid-back spot named after the movie filmed here. Try the seafood pizza or the lobster roll—they're both hits. Finish the night with a cocktail by the water as you watch the boats drift in and out of the bay.

Insider Tip: Ask your waiter about the local rum punch—it's strong but oh-so-delicious.

Day 4: Explore the Northern Coast

Morning: Visit Pigeon Island National Park
Today is all about exploring the north. Start with a visit to Pigeon Island National Park, where you can hike up to the fort for panoramic views or just chill on one of the quiet beaches. It's a great mix of history, nature, and relaxation.

Afternoon: Lunch and Shopping in Rodney Bay
Head back to Rodney Bay for lunch at Spice of India. The flavors here are incredible—go for the butter chicken or the lamb vindaloo. After lunch, take a stroll through the shops at Baywalk Mall. Pick up some souvenirs or treat yourself to a little retail therapy.

Evening: Beach BBQ at Reduit Beach
Finish the day with a beach BBQ at Reduit Beach. Some hotels and beach bars offer BBQ nights with live music, grilled seafood, and plenty of dancing. It's the perfect way to experience the island's laid-back nightlife.

Insider Tip: Try the grilled snapper—it's fresh, flavorful, and pairs perfectly with a cold Piton beer.

Day 5: Relax, Reflect, and Say Goodbye

Morning: Spa Morning or Beach Time
It's your last day, so let's take it easy. Book a morning spa treatment at your hotel or head to the beach for a final swim. If you're staying near Marigot Bay, grab a kayak and paddle around the calm waters—it's a peaceful way to say goodbye to the island.

Afternoon: Lunch at a Local Favorite
Before you head to the airport, stop for lunch at Golden Taste in Gros Islet. It's a local favorite, known for its authentic St. Lucian dishes. Order

the green fig and saltfish (the national dish) and savor every bite.

Evening: Depart for Home
Your 5-day adventure in St. Lucia has come to an end. Pack up your bags, double-check your souvenirs, and head to the airport. Reflect on your amazing experiences as you take one last look at the stunning Caribbean scenery from your plane window.

Insider Tip: Leave a little extra room in your suitcase for last-minute goodies from the airport's duty-free shop—St. Lucian chocolate and rum make great gifts!

C. Sample 7-Day Itinerary

Day 1: Arrival and Beach Bliss

Morning: Touchdown in Paradise
Welcome to St. Lucia! After arriving at Hewanorra International Airport (UVF) or George F.L. Charles Airport (SLU), grab a taxi or transfer to your hotel. Check-in, freshen up, and take a deep breath—you've made it!

Afternoon: Relax at Vigie Beach
Ease into your trip with some beach time at Vigie Beach, close to Castries. It's the perfect spot to relax, unwind, and shake off that travel fatigue. Sink your toes in the sand, grab a drink from a

beach bar, and let the Caribbean vibes work their magic.

Evening: Dinner in Rodney Bay
For your first night, head to Spice of India in Rodney Bay. The flavors here are bold and delicious—a great introduction to St. Lucia's vibrant culinary scene. Try the butter chicken or lamb vindaloo, paired with a tropical cocktail.

Insider Tip: If you're up for it, check out Rodney Bay's lively bars and nightlife scene after dinner.

Day 2: Explore the Pitons and Soufrière

Morning: Hike or View the Gros Piton
Get an early start and make your way to Soufrière for a hike up Gros Piton. This challenging hike takes you to the top of one of St. Lucia's iconic mountains with views that will take your breath away. If you'd prefer a less intense morning, you can drive to a scenic viewpoint and admire the Pitons from below.

Afternoon: Lunch at Dasheene and Sulphur Springs
After your hike, stop by Dasheene at Ladera Resort for lunch. The restaurant has one of the best views on the island, and the food is fresh and locally inspired. Once you're refueled, head to the Sulphur Springs for a rejuvenating mud bath. Soak up the minerals and rinse off in the hot springs—your skin will feel fantastic.

Evening: Dinner in Soufrière
Wind down the day with dinner at Orlando's Restaurant in Soufrière. The farm-to-table menu is a celebration of Caribbean flavors, and you'll get a real taste of St. Lucia's culinary creativity.

Insider Tip: Take a stroll along Soufrière's waterfront after dinner for a peaceful end to your action-packed day.

Day 3: Sailing and Snorkeling Adventure

Morning: Sail Along the Coast
Book a half-day sailing excursion along St. Lucia's scenic west coast. Most tours leave from Rodney Bay or Marigot Bay and take you past beautiful beaches, coastal cliffs, and those iconic Piton views. Bring your camera and enjoy the sea breeze!

Afternoon: Snorkeling at Anse Chastanet
Anchor at Anse Chastanet Beach and dive into the clear waters for some snorkeling. The reefs here are alive with vibrant fish and coral, making it one of the best snorkeling spots on the island. If you'd rather relax, just lounge on the beach and soak up the sun.

Evening: Casual Dinner at Marigot Bay
Head to Marigot Bay and grab a laid-back dinner at Doolittle's Restaurant. The relaxed atmosphere and waterfront views make it the

perfect spot to end the day. Try the seafood pizza or the lobster roll, and kick back with a rum punch.

Insider Tip: Stay a little longer for the sunset—it's magical from Marigot Bay.

Day 4: Cultural Day in Castries

Morning: Castries Market and Cathedral
Spend the morning exploring Castries Market, where you'll find everything from fresh produce and spices to handcrafted souvenirs. Chat with local vendors, taste tropical fruits, and pick up some goodies to take home. Then, head over to the Cathedral of the Immaculate Conception for a bit of island history and beautiful architecture.

Afternoon: Pigeon Island National Park
After a bite to eat, make your way to Pigeon Island National Park. Hike up to the old fort for stunning panoramic views of the ocean and coastline, then unwind on the beach below. It's a great mix of history and nature, all in one beautiful spot.

Evening: Dinner at The Coal Pot
Wrap up your cultural day with a delicious meal at The Coal Pot in Castries. This waterfront restaurant is known for its fresh seafood and local flavors. Try the Creole shrimp or catch of the day, paired with a glass of wine or a cold Piton beer.

Day 5: Relaxation Day in Rodney Bay

Morning: Spa Day or Chill on Reduit Beach
You're halfway through the week, so it's time to relax! Book a morning spa treatment at one of the nearby resorts, or head to Reduit Beach in Rodney Bay for a lazy day in the sun. Rent a lounger, dip in the sea, and let yourself fully unwind.

Afternoon: Lunch and Shopping at Baywalk Mall
When you're ready for a break from the sun, head to Baywalk Mall for some shopping and lunch. Browse the stores, pick up souvenirs, and grab a bite at one of the casual eateries. It's a fun way to spend a laid-back afternoon.

Evening: Sunset Dinner at Buzz Seafood & Grill
For dinner, try Buzz Seafood & Grill in Rodney Bay. The food is excellent, and the ambiance is relaxed and inviting. Order the seafood platter or the steak, and watch the sun dip below the horizon as you toast to your time in paradise.

Day 6: Day Trip to Martinique or the Grenadines

Full Day: Island Hopping Adventure
With seven days, you've got time for a day trip! Catch a ferry to Martinique for a taste of French-Caribbean culture, or book a boat tour to the Grenadines, known for their untouched

beauty and vibrant marine life. Each offers its own unique charm and adventure, so pick the one that excites you most.

Evening: Return to St. Lucia
After a full day exploring neighboring islands, return to St. Lucia. Enjoy a relaxing evening and unwind after an adventurous day.

Insider Tip: Bring your passport if you're heading to Martinique, as it's a French territory.

Day 7: Final Day and Farewell Dinner

Morning: Kayaking in Marigot Bay
For your last morning, take a peaceful kayak trip around Marigot Bay. Paddle through the calm waters, explore hidden coves, and take in the views one last time. It's the perfect way to say goodbye to the island.

Afternoon: Lunch and Final Beach Time
Head back to your favorite beach from earlier in the week or try a new one. Enjoy a final swim, soak up the sun, and take in the sights and sounds of St. Lucia.

Evening: Farewell Dinner at Cap Maison
For your last dinner, treat yourself to a meal at The Cliff at Cap in Cap Maison. This clifftop restaurant offers some of the best views on the island, and the food is absolutely delicious. Toast

to an unforgettable week as you watch the sun set over the Caribbean Sea.

D. Tips for Customizing Your Trip

1. Choose the Right Season for Your Vibe

Before diving into your activities, consider the best time to visit St. Lucia based on your travel style:

- <u>December to April:</u> This is the dry season and the peak travel period. It's the best time for guaranteed sunshine, but it's also busier and pricier. Perfect if you love festivals, beach parties, and vibrant island energy.
- <u>May to November:</u> The off-season brings fewer crowds and great deals on accommodations. Expect a bit of rain, but it usually comes in short, refreshing bursts. This is ideal if you're looking for a quieter, more laid-back experience.

<u>Pro Tip:</u> If you're visiting during Carnival (July), plan to join in the festivities—it's one of the biggest celebrations on the island!

2. Pick Your Perfect Base

Where you stay on the island can shape your entire experience. Here's how to decide:

- <u>The North (Rodney Bay, Gros Islet)</u>: This area is bustling with nightlife, restaurants, and beautiful beaches like Reduit Beach. It's great if you want to be close to the action, with easy access to shopping and lively bars.
- <u>The South (Soufrière, Vieux Fort)</u>: This is where you'll find the iconic Pitons, the Sulphur Springs, and lots of nature activities. It's a bit quieter, perfect for those who want to focus on hiking, snorkeling, and exploring the natural beauty of the island.

<u>Pro Tip:</u> Can't decide? Split your stay! Spend a few days in the north for the nightlife and then head south for relaxation and adventure.

3. Mix Up Your Activities: Adventure, Relaxation, and Culture

Don't feel like you have to stick to one type of experience—St. Lucia offers a little bit of everything, so mix it up! Here are some ideas to tailor your trip:

- <u>For Adventure Lovers:</u> Add more hikes (like the Tet Paul Nature Trail), zip-lining through the rainforest, or scuba diving at Anse Cochon. You can even try kitesurfing in Vieux Fort if you're visiting during the windy season.
- <u>For Foodies:</u> Book a food tour in Castries to sample local favorites like green fig and

saltfish or cassava bread. Take a cooking class to learn how to make your own Creole dishes, or visit a cocoa plantation for a chocolate-making experience.
- For Relaxation Seekers: Swap out some activities for spa days or quiet beach time. Book a massage at the Rainforest Spa in Sugar Beach or relax in a hammock at Anse Mamin. Treat yourself—you're on vacation!
- For History Buffs: Spend more time exploring cultural sites like Pigeon Island National Park or the La Sikwi Sugar Mill in Soufrière. Join a guided heritage tour to learn about the island's colonial past and rich Creole culture.

Pro Tip: Leave a little free time in your schedule. The best experiences often come from spontaneous moments, like discovering a hidden beach or stumbling upon a local street party.

4. Tailor Your Transportation

Getting around St. Lucia can be half the adventure. Here's how to decide what's best for you:
- Rent a Car: If you love the freedom to explore at your own pace, renting a car is a fantastic option. Just remember, they drive on the left side of the road here! A 4x4 vehicle is recommended if you plan to

visit off-the-beaten-path spots or tackle some of the steeper, winding roads.
- <u>Take Taxis:</u> Taxis are convenient and give you a chance to chat with local drivers, who often double as informal tour guides. Just agree on the fare before you start the ride since taxis aren't metered.
- <u>Book Guided Tours</u>: If you want a stress-free experience, opt for guided tours. You'll get expert insights and won't have to worry about directions or logistics. This is a great choice for activities like sailing, snorkeling, or visiting the Pitons.

<u>Pro Tip:</u> For a unique experience, book a private driver for a day. They can take you to hidden gems and local spots you might not find on your own.

5. Plan Your Budget

St. Lucia has options for every budget, so it's all about balancing your splurges and savings:
- <u>Splurge On:</u> Unique experiences like a sunset cruise, dining at a top restaurant like The Cliff at Cap, or a stay at one of the island's luxury resorts (even if it's just for one night).
- <u>Save On:</u> Opt for local eats at roadside food stalls or the Castries Market. You'll get a taste of authentic St. Lucian cuisine without the high price tag. Also, take

advantage of free activities like hiking local trails or exploring the public beaches.

Pro Tip: Check for package deals at hotels, especially during the off-season. You can often find great offers that include meals, excursions, or spa treatments.

6. Leave Room for Local Experiences

St. Lucia's charm isn't just in its stunning landscapes—it's in the people and local culture. Make time for experiences that help you connect with the island:
- Attend a Local Festival: From the St. Lucia Jazz Festival in May to Jounen Kwéyòl (Creole Day) in October, these events are vibrant celebrations of the island's culture.
- Visit a Fishing Village: Spend an afternoon in a village like Canaries or Dennery, where you can watch fishermen bring in the day's catch and try fresh seafood right on the spot.
- Learn a Few Phrases in Kwéyòl: The local Creole language is fun to learn and will earn you big smiles from the locals. Simple phrases like "Bonjou!" (Good morning) and "Mesi!" (Thank you) go a long way.

<u>Pro Tip:</u> Ask locals for their favorite spots to eat or swim—they often know the best hidden gems that aren't in the guidebooks.

100

Chapter 6: Top Attractions and Must-See Sights

A. The Pitons

If you're looking for the one sight that truly captures the spirit of St. Lucia, it's got to be the Pitons. These towering volcanic spires are the island's most famous natural landmarks and a UNESCO World Heritage Site. Whether you're hiking up their steep trails or simply gazing at them from the beach, the Pitons are sure to leave you awestruck. Ready to explore? Let's dive into what makes these peaks so special and how you can experience them up close.

What Are the Pitons?

The Pitons are two massive volcanic plugs—Gros Piton and Petit Piton—rising dramatically from the Caribbean Sea on St. Lucia's southwestern coast. They stand like majestic sentinels, framing the horizon and creating an unforgettable silhouette against the sky. Gros Piton, the larger of the two, reaches a height of 2,618 feet (798 meters), while Petit Piton stands at 2,438 feet (743 meters). These volcanic peaks are covered in lush rainforest and home to diverse wildlife, making them a must-visit for nature lovers and thrill-seekers alike.

Fun Fact: The Pitons are featured on St. Lucia's national flag as symbols of strength and resilience. They're a true point of pride for the island!

Best Ways to Experience the Pitons

Whether you're up for a challenging hike or prefer a more relaxed approach, there are several ways to enjoy the beauty of the Pitons:

1. Hike Gros Piton:
If you're looking for an adventure, hiking up Gros Piton is a bucket-list experience. The trail is steep and challenging, but it's well-marked and guided, making it suitable for most fitness levels. Your hike will start in the quaint village of Fond Gens Libre, which translates to "Valley of the Free People," a nod to the area's history as a refuge for escaped enslaved people. Along the way, your guide will point out medicinal plants and share stories of the island's past.

- **Trail Length:** About 4 miles (6.4 km) round trip
- **Hiking Time:** 3-5 hours, depending on your pace
- **Difficulty:** Moderate to strenuous (bring good hiking shoes and plenty of water!)
- **Cost:** Guided hikes start at around $50 USD per person

Pro Tip: Start your hike early in the morning to avoid the midday heat and get the best views from the top before clouds roll in.

2. Sail Around the Pitons:
Not in the mood for a strenuous hike? No problem! You can still experience the stunning beauty of the Pitons by sea. Book a catamaran or sailing tour from Marigot Bay or Rodney Bay and enjoy a leisurely cruise along St. Lucia's coast. The view of the Pitons from the water is breathtaking, especially at sunset when the sky turns shades of pink and gold. It's the perfect way to relax and take in the scenery.

- **Duration:** Most sailing tours last 2-4 hours
- **Cost:** Prices range from $75 - $150 USD per person, depending on the tour
- **Bonus:** Many tours include snorkeling stops at Anse Chastanet, where you can explore vibrant coral reefs.

Pro Tip: Bring your camera or smartphone with a good zoom lens—the Pitons are incredibly photogenic, and you'll want to capture the moment!

3. Enjoy the View from a Beachfront Restaurant
For a more laid-back experience, grab a table at a beachfront restaurant like Dasheene at Ladera Resort. This spot offers one of the best views of the Pitons on the island, and you can enjoy it while sipping on a tropical cocktail or digging into a delicious Creole meal. It's a great way to experience the iconic peaks without breaking a sweat.

4. Snorkeling at the Base of the Pitons
The waters surrounding the Pitons are part of the Pitons Management Area, a marine reserve teeming with underwater life. Head to Sugar Beach or Anse Chastanet for some of the best snorkeling on the island. You'll see vibrant coral reefs, schools of tropical fish, and if you're lucky, a few friendly sea turtles. The crystal-clear water and dramatic backdrop make it a snorkeling experience you won't forget.

Tips for Visiting the Pitons

- <u>Bring Water and Snacks:</u> Whether you're hiking or taking a tour, it's always a good idea to stay hydrated and have a light snack on hand.
- <u>Wear Sunscreen and Bug Spray:</u> The sun can be strong, especially during the hike, and the rainforest is home to plenty of

mosquitoes. Protect yourself so you can focus on the views.
- <u>Book a Guide for the Hike</u>: While it's possible to hike Gros Piton without a guide, having a local guide enhances the experience with their knowledge of the terrain, history, and plant life.
- <u>Timing Matters:</u> If you're planning to hike, go early in the morning to avoid the heat. For sunset cruises, book in advance as they tend to fill up quickly.

How to Get There

The Pitons are located near the town of Soufrière on the island's west coast. If you're staying in Rodney Bay or Castries, it's about a 1.5-hour drive. You can either rent a car and drive yourself or join a guided tour that includes transportation.

- <u>By Car:</u> Drive south along the west coast road, following signs for Soufrière.
- <u>By Tour:</u> Many tours departing from major resorts include a stop at the Pitons.

B. Soufrière Volcano and Sulphur Springs

Ready to get up close and personal with a real-life volcano? The Soufrière Volcano, also known as the Sulphur Springs, is one of St. Lucia's most famous attractions and a must-visit on your trip. Imagine driving right into the crater of an active volcano, feeling the heat rise from the ground, and soaking in mineral-rich mud baths that will leave your skin feeling amazing. Let's explore what makes this spot so special and why you absolutely can't miss it.

What Is the Soufrière Volcano?

The Soufrière Volcano is a dormant volcano located near the town of Soufrière on the island's southwest coast. It's known as the world's only drive-in volcano, which means you can literally drive right into the crater! Here, you'll find boiling hot springs, steam vents, and bubbling mud pools. The area gets its name, Sulphur Springs, from the strong smell of sulfur (think rotten eggs) that comes from the volcanic gases.

Fun Fact: The name "Soufrière" comes from the French word for sulfur, highlighting the area's volcanic history. Locals also call the volcano the "Sleeping Giant," as it hasn't erupted since the 18th century.

Top Things to Do at the Sulphur Springs

1. Take a Guided Tour of the Volcano Crater

Start your visit with a guided tour of the Sulphur Springs Park, where you'll get a close look at the volcanic activity. Your guide will lead you through the crater, explaining the fascinating geology and history of the volcano. You'll see steam vents spewing hot sulfuric gases, pools of bubbling mud, and water boiling at temperatures over 340°F (170°C). It's like stepping into another world!

- <u>Tour Duration:</u> About 30-45 minutes
- <u>Cost:</u> Entry fees are around $10 USD per person, with guided tours included.
- <u>What to Bring:</u> Wear comfortable shoes—you'll be walking on uneven, rocky terrain. And don't forget your camera; the landscape is surreal!

<u>Pro Tip:</u> Listen for the sizzling sound of the boiling water—it's a reminder that the volcanic activity is very much alive!

2. Enjoy a Mud Bath:

After your tour, it's time to get messy in the best way possible. The Sulphur Springs Mud Baths are a highlight of any visit. You'll slather yourself in warm, mineral-rich volcanic mud, which is said to have healing properties for the skin. Let the mud dry for a few minutes, then rinse off in the natural hot springs. It's a unique experience that leaves your skin feeling silky smooth and rejuvenated.

- <u>Cost</u>: The mud bath experience is included with your Sulphur Springs entry fee.
- <u>What to Bring</u>: A swimsuit you don't mind getting dirty (the mud can stain light-colored fabrics), a towel, and water shoes for comfort.
- <u>Pro Tip:</u> Apply a second layer of mud and let it dry completely before rinsing—it's like a natural face mask, but for your whole body!

3. Take a Dip in the Piton Falls

If you're looking for another spot to soak and relax, head to Piton Falls, just a short drive from the Sulphur Springs. The waterfall cascades into a series of hot and cold pools, surrounded by lush rainforest. It's the perfect place to unwind after your mud bath and enjoy a peaceful moment in nature.

- <u>Entry Fee:</u> About $3 USD per person

- Pro Tip: Visit early in the morning or late in the afternoon to avoid crowds. You might have the falls all to yourself!

4. Explore Soufrière Town and Have Lunch

Once you've had your fill of the volcano, head back into the town of Soufrière for a bite to eat. There are plenty of local restaurants where you can try authentic St. Lucian dishes like green fig and saltfish or Creole-style seafood. It's a great way to refuel after your morning of exploring.

- Recommended Spot: Check out Fedo's Restaurant, a local favorite known for its hearty Caribbean meals and friendly service.

The History Behind the Sulphur Springs

The volcanic activity in Soufrière dates back 200,000 years, shaping the landscape of St. Lucia as we know it today. The last major eruption occurred in the late 1700s, and since then, the volcano has remained dormant, although the hot springs and steam vents are constant reminders of its fiery past. The area was initially settled by the French, who were fascinated by the healing properties of the mineral waters and often used the springs as a natural spa.

- Fun Fact: During the colonial era, the Sulphur Springs were a popular spot for the island's wealthy residents, who believed the waters could cure various ailments, from skin conditions to arthritis.

Tips for Visiting the Sulphur Springs

- Avoid Peak Times: The Sulphur Springs can get busy, especially on weekends and during cruise ship season. Plan your visit early in the morning or late in the afternoon for a more peaceful experience.
- Stay Hydrated: The combination of hot springs and sulfuric fumes can be dehydrating, so bring plenty of water.
- Keep an Eye on Your Jewelry: The sulfur in the water can tarnish certain metals, so it's best to leave your favorite rings and necklaces back at the hotel.

How to Get There

The Sulphur Springs are located about 10 minutes from the town of Soufrière. If you're staying in Rodney Bay or Castries, it's roughly a 1.5-hour drive along the west coast. You can easily rent a car, hire a taxi, or join a guided tour that includes transportation.

- By Car: Follow the main road south to Soufrière and look for signs to the Sulphur Springs.
- By Tour: Many local tour operators offer half-day and full-day trips that include

stops at the Sulphur Springs, Piton Falls, and other nearby attractions.

C. Pigeon Island National Park

Hey there! If you're looking for a place where history meets stunning scenery, Pigeon Island National Park is the spot. This 44-acre island-turned-peninsula on the northwest coast of St. Lucia is a must-visit for anyone wanting to dive into the island's fascinating past while soaking up breathtaking views of the Caribbean Sea. Ready to explore? Let's take a walk through the trails, discover ancient ruins, and relax on beautiful beaches.

A Little History

Pigeon Island has a colorful past that dates back centuries. It was once a hideout for notorious pirates who used the island's strategic location to launch attacks on passing ships. In the 18th century, the British military took control of Pigeon Island, building forts to keep an eye on the French, who were stationed on nearby

Martinique. The island became a key battleground during the battles between the French and the British for control of the Caribbean. Today, you can still see the remnants of these old forts and military barracks, giving you a glimpse into the island's storied history.

- Fun Fact: The island is named after the large number of passenger pigeons that once roosted here. Unfortunately, the species has since become extinct, but the island's name remains a tribute to its former inhabitants.

Top Things to Do at Pigeon Island National Park

1. Hike Up to Fort Rodney for Panoramic Views
Your first stop should be Fort Rodney, a historic fort perched atop a hill with incredible 360-degree views. The hike up is short but steep, so wear sturdy shoes and take your time. Once you reach the top, you'll be rewarded with sweeping views of Rodney Bay, the sparkling Caribbean Sea, and on a clear day, you can even spot the island of Martinique in the distance. It's the perfect spot to snap some photos and take in the beauty of St. Lucia.

- Hiking Time: About 20-30 minutes to reach the top
- Difficulty: Easy to moderate (bring water and take it slow if it's hot)

Pro Tip: Go early in the morning or late in the afternoon for the best light and fewer crowds.

2. Explore the Historic Ruins

Pigeon Island is dotted with historic ruins that give you a glimpse into its past as a military stronghold. Wander through the remains of old barracks, powder magazines, and officer quarters. There's even a small museum near the entrance that offers more insights into the island's history. It's like stepping back in time, and the information boards provide fascinating details about the battles fought here.

- Museum Entry: Included with your park admission fee

Pro Tip: Take a moment to imagine what life was like for the soldiers stationed here in the 18th century—watching the sea for enemy ships and living in the rugged barracks.

3. Relax on the Beaches

After your hike and history lesson, it's time to hit the beach. Pigeon Island has two lovely beaches with calm, turquoise waters. They're great for swimming, sunbathing, or simply enjoying a picnic under the shade of a palm tree. The sand is soft, the water is warm, and the setting is peaceful—it's everything you want in a Caribbean beach experience.

- Beach Facilities: There are restrooms, picnic tables, and a small snack bar nearby.

Pro Tip: Bring your snorkeling gear! The clear waters

D. Diamond Falls and Botanical Gardens

Hey, nature lover! If you're craving a serene escape surrounded by lush greenery, vibrant flowers, and soothing sounds of cascading water, Diamond Falls and Botanical Gardens is your paradise. Nestled near Soufrière, this beautiful garden offers a little bit of everything—stunning plant life, therapeutic mineral baths, and one of the most colorful waterfalls you'll ever see. Let's dive into what makes this spot a must-visit on your St. Lucia adventure.

A Brief History

Diamond Falls and Botanical Gardens is more than just a pretty place; it's steeped in history. The gardens date back to the 18th century, when King Louis XVI of France granted this land to the

Devaux family, who turned it into a retreat for French soldiers. The mineral-rich waters in the baths were thought to have healing properties, and over time, the site transformed into a lush tropical garden open to the public. Today, the Devaux family still manages the property, welcoming visitors to experience its natural beauty and historical charm.

- Fun Fact: The minerals in the water come from the nearby volcanic activity, which gives Diamond Falls its unique, ever-changing colors. The waterfall's vibrant hues are due to the minerals, which can range from yellow to green to purplish, depending on the mineral concentration at the time.

Top Things to Do at Diamond Falls and Botanical Gardens

1. Marvel at the Diamond Falls: A Natural Wonder

One of the main attractions here is, of course, Diamond Falls. It's not just any waterfall—its waters are infused with minerals from the island's volcanic activity, creating a beautiful cascade with colors that change throughout the year. The minerals give the waterfall a shimmering, almost magical appearance, making it a picture-perfect spot.

- Viewing Area: There's a designated area for visitors to admire and photograph the falls, as swimming is not allowed.
- Best Time to Visit: The colors of the waterfall can vary depending on recent volcanic activity, so each visit can be unique.

Pro Tip: Visit in the morning for the best light and to enjoy the falls before it gets crowded.

2. Explore the Botanical Gardens: A Feast for the Senses

The Botanical Gardens are a haven for plant lovers, with a vibrant collection of tropical flowers, towering trees, and exotic plants. As you wander through the winding paths, you'll see hibiscus, heliconias, ginger lilies, and many more varieties of blooms that fill the air with their sweet fragrance. The gardens are meticulously maintained and provide a peaceful place to explore and connect with nature.

- Highlights: Look out for rare plants like the Balisier and the Jade Vine, which are native to the Caribbean.
- Photography: Every corner of the gardens is bursting with color, so keep your camera handy for some stunning shots.

Pro Tip: Take your time and enjoy the garden's many benches and shaded spots—it's a great place to relax and just soak in the beauty around you.

3. Soak in the Mineral Baths: St. Lucia's Natural Spa

One of the most unique experiences at Diamond Falls and Botanical Gardens is the chance to soak in the mineral baths. These therapeutic baths are fed by natural springs, rich in minerals believed to have healing properties for the skin and body. The baths are located in a secluded area of the garden, offering a relaxing, almost spa-like experience surrounded by nature.

- Cost: Access to the mineral baths is around $7 USD in addition to the garden entrance fee.
- What to Bring: Wear a swimsuit and bring a towel. The mineral water can stain light-colored clothing, so it's best to avoid white.

Pro Tip: Soak for about 15-20 minutes to fully enjoy the soothing effects of the mineral water. Your skin will feel refreshed and rejuvenated!

4. Discover the Old Mill and Water Wheel: A Touch of History

The Old Mill and Water Wheel are relics from the 18th century and add a historical charm to the gardens. Once used to power the plantation's machinery, the water wheel is a fascinating piece of St. Lucia's history. It's a peaceful spot to sit and reflect, and the sound of the wheel turning with the flowing water adds to the garden's serene atmosphere.

- <u>Location:</u> Near the entrance to the gardens, the old mill and water wheel are easy to find and make for a great photo op.

<u>Pro Tip:</u> Ask one of the guides for a brief history of the water wheel—they're full of interesting stories and facts about the area's past.

Tips for Visiting Diamond Falls and Botanical Gardens

- <u>Entrance Fee:</u> Entry to the gardens is around $7 USD per person, with an additional fee for access to the mineral baths.
- <u>Guided Tours:</u> Guided tours are available and highly recommended if you want to learn more about the plants, history, and significance of the gardens. The guides are knowledgeable and bring the garden's story to life.
- <u>Wear Comfortable Shoes:</u> The garden paths are easy to navigate, but comfortable walking shoes will make exploring even more enjoyable.
- <u>Best Time to Visit:</u> Mornings are quieter, and the lighting is perfect for photos. Plus, you'll beat the midday crowds that often arrive with tour groups.

How to Get There

Diamond Falls and Botanical Gardens is located near Soufrière, making it easily accessible if you're staying in or around this area. If you're staying further north in places like Rodney Bay or Castries, it's about a 1.5-hour drive along scenic coastal roads.

- By Car: Follow signs to Soufrière and look for Diamond Falls and Botanical Gardens, located just outside the main town.
- By Taxi or Tour: Many tours include Diamond Falls as part of a full-day Soufrière excursion, which often includes stops at the Sulphur Springs and the Pitons as well.

E. Castries Market and Local Experiences

If you want to experience the real pulse of St. Lucia, there's no better place than Castries Market. This vibrant, bustling market is the beating heart of the island's capital city, offering everything from fresh produce and spices to handcrafted souvenirs and local street food. It's a sensory overload—in the best way possible. Ready to explore the sights, sounds, and flavors of St. Lucia like a local? Let's dive into what makes Castries Market a must-visit on your trip.

A Bit of History

Castries Market has been the island's main hub for trade and commerce since it opened in 1894. It's one of the oldest markets in the Caribbean and remains a vital part of daily life in St. Lucia. For more than a century, locals have come here to buy fresh produce, catch up on the latest gossip, and sell handmade crafts to visitors. It's a place where the island's culture, history, and community spirit come together in a colorful, lively setting.

- Fun Fact: In 2011, Castries Market was named one of the world's top 10 food markets by National Geographic. It's a must-visit for foodies and anyone interested in authentic local experiences.

Top Things to Do at Castries Market

1. Shop for Fresh Produce and Local Delicacies
The first thing you'll notice as you enter the market is the vibrant array of fresh fruits and vegetables. From juicy mangoes and sweet

pineapples to exotic starfruit and soursop, you'll find a variety of tropical produce you might not see back home. Don't be shy—vendors are usually happy to let you sample their goods. It's the perfect opportunity to try something new and learn about the island's agriculture.

- Must-Try Items: Pick up some fresh bananas (St. Lucia is known for its sweet bananas), local avocados, or a bag of tamarind balls for a sweet and tangy snack.

Pro Tip: Bring cash in small bills, as many vendors don't accept cards. It's also a great way to support local farmers directly.

2. Spice It Up: Discover Local Spices and Flavors
As you wander deeper into the market, you'll come across stalls filled with fragrant spices and seasonings. St. Lucian cuisine is all about bold, rich flavors, and this is your chance to bring some of those tastes home. Look for bags of cinnamon, nutmeg, bay leaves, and the island's famous green seasoning, a blend of herbs and spices used in almost every local dish.

- Recommended Purchase: Grab a pack of local cocoa sticks—these are used to make traditional St. Lucian hot chocolate. The flavor is rich, deep, and unlike anything you've tasted before.

Pro Tip: Ask the vendors for their favorite ways to use the spices—they often have great cooking tips and recipes to share.

3. Taste the Street Food
Castries Market is a foodie's paradise, with plenty of street food vendors offering tasty bites you won't want to miss. Try a bake and saltfish, a local breakfast staple made with fried dough and salted cod. For lunch, go for a plate of bouyon, a hearty stew made with meat, vegetables, and dumplings, or grab a roti, filled with curried meat or vegetables.

- Must-Try Drink: Don't leave without sampling a fresh coconut water or a glass of locally made mauby, a refreshing drink made from the bark of the mauby tree with a slightly bitter taste.

Pro Tip: Try to visit on a Saturday morning—the market is at its liveliest, and you'll find the best selection of fresh food.

4. Shop for Souvenirs: Handicrafts and Local Art
Looking for a special keepsake from your trip? The market has plenty of vendors selling handmade crafts, from woven baskets and straw hats to beautiful

Chapter 7: Beaches of St. Lucia

A. The Best Beaches for Relaxation

1. Reduit Beach

Let's start with the classic choice—Reduit Beach in Rodney Bay. This is one of St. Lucia's most popular and well-loved beaches, and for good reason. It's a long stretch of golden sand with calm, clear waters, perfect for swimming and relaxing. The beach is lined with bars, restaurants, and resorts, giving you plenty of options for food and drinks. It's a lively spot, but it's big enough that you can always find a quiet corner to lay down your towel and soak up the sun.

- Location: Rodney Bay, on the northwest coast

- Entry Fee: Free public access
- Facilities: Public restrooms, beach chair rentals, and plenty of nearby bars and restaurants

Pro Tip: Arrive early to snag a good spot, especially if you're visiting during peak season. Parking is available but can fill up quickly on weekends.

2. Anse Chastanet

For a more secluded and picturesque beach experience, head to Anse Chastanet near Soufrière. This beach is part of the Anse Chastanet Resort, but it's open to the public. The sand here is darker, thanks to the volcanic origin of the area, and the water is crystal clear, making it an incredible spot for snorkeling. The beach has a quieter vibe and offers stunning views of the Pitons.

- Location: Near Soufrière, on the southwest coast
- Entry Fee: Free public access (parking at the resort may cost around $10 USD)
- Facilities: Snorkeling gear rentals, a beachfront restaurant, and restrooms

Pro Tip: Bring your own snorkel gear if you have it—renting can get pricey. The coral reefs here are some of the best on the island.

3. Sugar Beach (Jalousie Beach)

Sugar Beach, also known as Jalousie Beach, is a slice of paradise nestled between the iconic Gros Piton and Petit Piton. This beach is part of the luxury Sugar Beach Resort, but the main beach area is open to the public. The sand is soft and white, and the turquoise water is calm, perfect for swimming. The dramatic views of the Pitons make this one of the most photogenic beaches on the island.

- <u>Location</u>: Between Gros Piton and Petit Piton, near Soufrière
- <u>Entry Fee:</u> Free public access, but there's a $50 USD parking fee if you drive to the resort. Alternatively, you can take a water taxi from Soufrière for about $20 USD round trip.
- <u>Facilities</u>: Sun lounger rentals, a beach bar, and restrooms (loungers can cost around $50 USD for the day)

<u>Pro Tip:</u> Arrive by water taxi to avoid the hefty parking fee, and get there early if you want a sun lounger—they go fast!

4. Pigeon Island Beach

Pigeon Island Beach is part of Pigeon Island National Park, offering a mix of history and beautiful beach scenery. This spot is perfect if you want a bit of culture with your beach time. The sand is soft, the water is calm, and the beach offers plenty of shaded areas. It's a great place to relax after exploring the old forts and hiking trails in the park.

- <u>Location</u>: Pigeon Island, near Gros Islet
- <u>Entry Fee</u>: The entrance fee to Pigeon Island National Park is about $10 USD per person
- <u>Facilities</u>: Restrooms, picnic tables, snorkeling rentals, and the Jambe de Bois Café

<u>Pro Tip:</u> Pack a picnic and enjoy it under the trees—there are plenty of shaded spots that make for a great lunch break.

5. Marigot Bay Beach

Marigot Bay Beach is a small, secluded beach in one of the most beautiful bays in the Caribbean. It's a great spot for a quiet day of relaxation away from the crowds. The beach itself is small but lovely, with calm waters that are perfect for swimming and paddleboarding. You'll also find a few charming waterfront bars where you can grab a drink and enjoy the view.

- <u>Location</u>: Marigot Bay, on the west coast
- <u>Entry Fee:</u> Free public access, but taking a water taxi from Marigot Bay Marina costs about $5 USD per person
- <u>Facilities</u>: Beach bars, restrooms, and paddleboard rentals

<u>Pro Tip:</u> The water taxi ride is part of the experience—enjoy the scenic trip across the bay.

Tips for Enjoying St. Lucia's Relaxing Beaches

- Bring Cash: Many beach vendors and rental services only accept cash, so it's good to have small bills on hand.
- Stay Hydrated: The sun can be intense, so keep a bottle of water with you, especially if you plan on spending the whole day at the beach.
- Respect the Environment: Some of these beaches are part of protected areas, so remember to take your trash with you and be mindful of the local wildlife.
- Be Cautious with Valuables: While St. Lucia is generally safe, it's always a good idea to keep an eye on your belongings or leave valuables at your hotel.

Getting There: Transportation Tips

- By Car: Renting a car gives you the flexibility to explore multiple beaches. Just be aware that parking can be limited, especially at popular spots like Reduit Beach.
- By Taxi: Taxis are a convenient option, and many drivers offer beach tours where they'll take you to several spots in one day. Make sure to agree on the fare before starting your trip.
- By Water Taxi: For a unique experience, take a water taxi from Soufrière or

Marigot Bay. It's a fun and scenic way to reach the more secluded beaches.

B. Snorkeling and Diving Spots

1. Anse Chastanet

If you're looking for the best snorkeling experience in St. Lucia, Anse Chastanet is the place to be. This beach near Soufrière offers some of the island's most vibrant coral reefs, teeming with marine life. The waters are calm and clear, making it perfect for both beginners and experienced snorkelers. Just a few meters from the shore, you'll find a colorful underwater garden full of parrotfish, sergeant majors, and even the occasional stingray.

- Location: Near Soufrière, on the southwestern coast
- Entry Fee: Free public access (parking at the Anse Chastanet Resort may cost around $10 USD)
- Facilities: Snorkeling gear rentals, a beachfront restaurant, and restrooms
- What to See: Expect to see vibrant coral formations, butterflyfish, angelfish, and maybe even a sea turtle or two!

Pro Tip: Snorkel early in the morning for the clearest water and the best chance to see sea turtles.

Diving at Anse Chastanet:
If you're a certified diver, you can also explore the deeper sections of the reef with a dive tour from the Scuba St. Lucia Dive Shop. They offer guided dives that take you to incredible spots like the Anse Chastanet Wall, where you can see barrel sponges, seahorses, and barracuda.

2. Sugar Beach (Jalousie Beach)

For a unique snorkeling experience with a breathtaking backdrop, head to Sugar Beach, nestled between the towering Gros Piton and Petit Piton. This beach is part of the luxury Sugar Beach Resort, but the snorkeling area is open to the public. The coral reefs here are part of the Soufrière Marine Management Area, a protected zone that's home to a wide variety of fish and coral species.

- Location: Between Gros Piton and Petit Piton, near Soufrière
- Entry Fee: Free access to the snorkeling area, but parking at the resort is $50 USD (consider taking a water taxi from Soufrière for a cheaper and scenic option)
- Facilities: Snorkeling gear rentals, beach bar, sun loungers (extra fee), and restrooms
- What to See: Look out for trumpetfish, blue tangs, and large schools of sergeant majors swimming through the corals.

Pro Tip: Stick to the designated snorkeling area near the rocks on the right side of the beach—that's where you'll find the best coral and fish.

Diving at Sugar Beach:
Divers will love the Superman's Flight Dive Site, located just off the coast. It's a drift dive that follows the steep underwater slope of Petit Piton, offering sightings of vibrant corals, sponges, and larger fish like barracuda and snapper bit more off the beaten path, Anse Cochon is your go-to. This quiet, secluded beach is known for its clear waters and healthy coral reefs, making it a fantastic spot for snorkeling. The bay is home to a wide variety of marine life, including schools of colorful fish, squid, and even the occasional octopus.

- Location: Anse La Raye, on the west coast
- Entry Fee: Free public access (small fee for parking, around $5 USD)
- Facilities: Beach bar, snorkeling gear rentals, and restrooms
- What to See: The reef is teeming with life, including butterflyfish, moray eels, and spotted drum fish.

Pro Tip: Anse Cochon is a great spot for a picnic, so pack a lunch and enjoy a quiet day at the beach.

Diving at Anse Cochon:

The Anse Cochon Reef is a favorite among divers. It's a shallow reef, making it great for beginners. You can explore coral gardens, swim through schools of fish, and even spot some wrecks at deeper depths.

4. Pigeon Island National Park

For a mix of history and underwater adventure, head to Pigeon Island National Park. This historic site isn't just for exploring old forts—it's also a great place to snorkel. The waters around Pigeon Island are clear and calm, with plenty of fish and small coral formations close to shore. It's a fantastic spot for beginners and families.

- Location: Pigeon Island, near Gros Islet
- Entry Fee: $10 USD per person (park entry fee)
- Facilities: Restrooms, picnic areas, snorkeling rentals, and the Jambe de Bois Café
- What to See: Spot trumpetfish, wrasse, and colorful parrotfish swimming among the rocks and corals.

Pro Tip: Head to the right side of the beach for the best snorkeling—this is where the rocky areas create great habitats for fish.

5. Marigot Bay

If you prefer a more relaxed, scenic spot for snorkeling, check out Marigot Bay. This sheltered bay is calm and quiet, making it a great place to float along the surface and watch the marine life below. The water here is usually crystal clear, offering great visibility for spotting fish and small rays.

- <u>Location</u>: Marigot Bay, on the west coast
- <u>Entry Fee:</u> Free public access (water taxi from Marigot Bay Marina costs about $5 USD per person)
- <u>Facilities</u>: Beach bars, snorkeling gear rentals, and paddleboard rentals
- <u>What to See:</u> Expect to find rays gliding along the sandy bottom, schools of small fish, and occasional sightings of sea stars.

<u>Pro Tip:</u> Visit in the early morning or late afternoon for the calmest waters and the best snorkeling conditions.

Tips for Snorkeling and Diving in St. Lucia

- <u>Bring Your Own Gear:</u> While most spots offer rentals, bringing your own mask and snorkel guarantees a better fit and saves money.
- <u>Wear Reef-Safe Sunscreen:</u> Protect the marine life by using sunscreen that doesn't harm the coral reefs.
- <u>Check the Weather:</u> Strong currents and waves can make snorkeling more challenging. If the water looks rough, ask a local for advice before heading out.

- <u>Follow the Rules:</u> Many snorkeling and diving spots are part of protected marine areas. Respect the regulations—don't touch the coral or disturb the wildlife.

How to Book Your Dive or Snorkel Trip

Most hotels and resorts offer snorkeling and diving packages, or you can book directly with dive shops like Scuba St. Lucia or Dive Saint Lucia. Prices for guided snorkeling tours start at around $40 - $60 USD per person, while diving trips typically range from $100 - $150 USD, including equipment.

C. Hidden Gems

1. Anse Mamin

If you want to find a quiet spot near Soufrière that feels miles away from the tourist crowds, head to Anse Mamin. This hidden beach is just a short walk or boat ride from the more popular Anse Chastanet, but it offers a totally different vibe. Surrounded by lush jungle and coconut palms, Anse Mamin is a peaceful retreat with soft, dark volcanic sand and clear, turquoise waters. It's the perfect place to relax, snorkel, or enjoy a romantic picnic.

- <u>Location</u>: Near Soufrière, accessible via a 15-minute walk from Anse Chastanet
- <u>Entry Fee:</u> Free public access (a small fee for parking if you drive to Anse Chastanet)
- <u>Facilities</u>: A small beach bar (serving some of the best burgers on the island), restrooms, and sun lounger rentals
- <u>What to Do</u>: Snorkel along the rocks, explore the nearby jungle trails, or just lay back and enjoy the serene surroundings

<u>Pro Tip:</u> Bring cash if you plan to eat at the beach bar—try their famous "Jungle Burger" for a delicious treat after a swim.

2. Grande Anse

For those willing to venture a bit off the beaten path, Grande Anse is a true hidden gem on the rugged east coast of St. Lucia. This beach is remote and unspoiled, with strong waves, dramatic cliffs, and golden sand that stretches as far as the eye can see. It's not ideal for swimming due to the strong currents, but it's a stunning spot for a picnic, a beach walk, or a bit of solitude. It's also one of the best places on the island for spotting nesting sea turtles during the right season.

- <u>Location</u>: On the east coast, about a 45-minute drive from Castries
- <u>Entry Fee:</u> Free access, but there are no facilities or lifeguards, so come prepared

- **What to Do:** Explore the tide pools, watch the waves crash against the rocks, and keep an eye out for leatherback turtles nesting from March to August

Pro Tip: Visit during the week when it's even quieter. Pack plenty of water, snacks, and a sun hat—there's little shade here, and no vendors.

3. Anse La Voute

If you're looking for a beach where you might not see another soul all day, Anse La Voute is your spot. This remote, crescent-shaped beach on the northern coast of St. Lucia is hard to find, but it's worth the effort. The beach is lined with palm trees and has crystal-clear water, making it a perfect place for a quiet swim or a relaxing afternoon in the sun. It's a bit of a trek to get here, but the seclusion and pristine beauty are well worth it.

- **Location:** Northern coast, near Cap Estate (accessible by a rough dirt road—4x4 recommended)
- **Entry Fee:** Free public access
- **Facilities:** None—this is a completely natural, undeveloped beach, so bring everything you need
- **What to Do:** Swim in the clear waters, relax on the sand, and enjoy the peaceful surroundings

Pro Tip: This beach is best for those looking for a true adventure. Make sure you have a good vehicle (or a local guide) to navigate the rough roads leading here.

4. Malgretoute Beach

Located just south of Soufrière, Malgretoute Beach is a quiet, local favorite that offers stunning views of Gros Piton. It's a small, pebbly beach with calm waters, perfect for a relaxing swim or a peaceful spot to watch the sunset. It's often overlooked by tourists, making it a great choice for those who want to avoid the crowds and enjoy a more authentic St. Lucian experience.

- Location: Near Soufrière, just south of the town
- Entry Fee: Free public access
- Facilities: A small snack bar, basic restrooms, and kayak rentals available
- What to Do: Swim, sunbathe, and take in the incredible view of Gros Piton. You can also rent a kayak and paddle out for an even better view of the mountain.

Pro Tip: Visit in the late afternoon for a stunning view of the sunset behind Gros Piton—it's a magical experience.

Tips for Exploring Hidden Beaches in St. Lucia

- Bring Your Own Supplies: Most of these hidden gems are undeveloped, so pack snacks, water, sunscreen, and anything else you might need for the day.
- Check the Tides: Some of these beaches, like Grande Anse, can have strong currents. Check with locals about the best time to visit, especially if you plan to swim.
- Wear Sturdy Shoes: Getting to these off-the-beaten-path beaches often involves a bit of hiking or walking on rough terrain. Sturdy sandals or water shoes are a good idea.
- Respect the Environment: These secluded beaches are part of St. Lucia's natural beauty. Take all your trash with you, and be mindful of any wildlife you might encounter.

How to Get to These Hidden Beaches

- By Car: Renting a car gives you the freedom to explore these less-accessible spots. A 4x4 vehicle is recommended for some of the more remote beaches like Anse La Voute.
- By Taxi or Local Guide: Hiring a local guide or taking a taxi is a great option if you're not comfortable navigating the

island's rougher roads. Plus, local guides often know the best hidden spots.
- <u>By Boat:</u> Some of these beaches, like Anse Mamin, can be easily accessed by boat. Taking a water taxi from Soufrière is a fun and scenic way to reach them.

Chapter 8: Outdoor Adventures and Activities

A. Hiking and Nature Trails

1. Gros Piton Trail

If you're up for a challenge, the Gros Piton Trail is the ultimate St. Lucian adventure. Gros Piton, one of the island's iconic volcanic peaks, stands at 2,619 feet (798 meters) and offers hikers a chance to conquer its steep slopes. The trail takes you through lush rainforest, past giant ferns and flowering plants, and up rocky sections where you'll need to scramble a bit. It's a tough hike, but the view from the top is worth every step—you'll be rewarded with sweeping panoramas of the island and the Caribbean Sea.

- Difficulty: Moderate to challenging (not recommended for beginners)

- <u>Duration:</u> 4-5 hours round trip
- <u>Trailhead:</u> The hike starts in the village of Fond Gens Libre, about a 15-minute drive from Soufrière
- <u>Entry Fee:</u> $50 USD per person (includes a mandatory local guide)
- <u>What to Bring:</u> Sturdy hiking shoes, plenty of water, sunscreen, and a camera for those epic views

<u>Pro Tip:</u> Start your hike early in the morning to avoid the midday heat, and don't forget to bring a hat—it gets sunny at the top!

2. Tet Paul Nature Trail

Looking for a shorter, easier hike that still offers incredible views? The Tet Paul Nature Trail is perfect for you. This trail is located near Soufrière and is part of the Pitons Management Area, a UNESCO World Heritage Site. It's a relatively easy walk that takes you through a small farm, past local medicinal plants, and up to a lookout point with breathtaking views of both Gros Piton and Petit Piton. The trail is well-maintained and guided tours are available, making it a great choice for families or those who want a more relaxed hike.

- <u>Difficulty:</u> Easy to moderate (suitable for most fitness levels)
- <u>Duration:</u> 45 minutes to 1 hour
- <u>Entry Fee:</u> $10 USD per person

- **What to Bring:** Comfortable walking shoes, water, and a camera for the incredible photo opportunities

Pro Tip: Don't skip the guided tour—the local guides are knowledgeable and will teach you about the plants, history, and culture of the area.

3. Enbas Saut Waterfall Trail

For a true rainforest experience, head to the Enbas Saut Waterfall Trail in the Edmund Forest Reserve. This trail takes you deep into the jungle, where you'll be surrounded by towering trees, colorful tropical flowers, and the sounds of birds and tree frogs. The highlight of the hike is the Enbas Saut Waterfall, a beautiful cascade where you can take a refreshing dip. It's a moderately challenging hike with some steep sections, but the cool, misty air of the rainforest makes it a pleasant escape from the heat.

- **Difficulty:** Moderate (some steep sections and muddy areas)
- **Duration:** 2-3 hours round trip
- **Entry Fee:** $10 USD per person (guide recommended but not mandatory)
- **What to Bring:** Waterproof shoes, bug spray, and a towel if you plan to swim at the waterfall

Pro Tip: Wear long sleeves and pants to protect against mosquito bites, especially if you're hiking in the late afternoon.

4. Pigeon Island National Park

If you're looking for a mix of history and hiking, Pigeon Island National Park offers the best of both worlds. The trails here are relatively short and easy, but they take you up to the historic Fort Rodney, where you can explore old military ruins and enjoy panoramic views of the island and the Caribbean Sea. The park is filled with native plants and trees, and you might even spot a few local birds along the way. It's a great option for families or anyone who wants a shorter, scenic hike.

- <u>Difficulty</u>: Easy (short trails with gentle inclines)
- <u>Duration:</u> 1-2 hours depending on how much exploring you do
- <u>Entry Fee</u>: $10 USD per person
- <u>What to Bring:</u> Comfortable walking shoes, sunscreen, and a camera for the stunning views from the fort

<u>Pro Tip:</u> Bring a picnic lunch and enjoy it on the beach after your hike—the park has beautiful, shaded picnic areas perfect for relaxing.

5. Millet Bird Sanctuary Trail

For a unique hiking experience that's all about wildlife, check out the Millet Bird Sanctuary Trail. This trail is located in the Millet Forest Reserve and offers guided hikes focused on birdwatching. The sanctuary is home to several rare and endemic bird species, including the St. Lucia Parrot, the island's national bird. The hike itself is moderate and takes you through lush forest with plenty of opportunities to spot colorful birds, butterflies, and tropical plants.

- <u>Difficulty:</u> Moderate (with some steep sections)
- <u>Duration:</u> 2 hours round trip
- <u>Entry Fee:</u> $15 USD per person (includes a guided tour)
- <u>What to Bring:</u> Binoculars, a bird identification guide, and plenty of water

<u>Pro Tip:</u> The best time for birdwatching is early in the morning. Book your tour in advance, as spots can fill up quickly, especially during peak season.

Tips for Hiking in St. Lucia

- <u>Wear Proper Footwear:</u> Trails can be muddy and uneven, so sturdy hiking shoes or boots are a must.
- <u>Stay Hydrated:</u> The tropical heat can be intense, especially on longer hikes. Bring plenty of water and take regular breaks.
- <u>Check the Weather:</u> Rain can make some trails slippery and challenging. If it looks like rain, consider rescheduling or opting for a shorter hike.
- <u>Respect the Wildlife:</u> St. Lucia's forests are home to many species of birds and

animals. Keep your distance and don't feed the wildlife.
- <u>Hire a Guide:</u> Local guides can enhance your experience with their knowledge of the island's history, flora, and fauna. Plus, they'll ensure you stay on the right path!

How to Book a Hiking Tour

Most hotels and resorts offer guided hiking tours, or you can book directly with tour operators like Rainforest Adventures St. Lucia or Island Routes. Prices for guided hikes range from $30 - $100 USD per person, depending on the trail and length of the hike. For a more personalized experience, consider hiring a private guide.

B. Water Sports

1. Kayaking

Kayaking is a fantastic way to experience St. Lucia's stunning coastline up close. Paddle through calm bays, navigate hidden caves, or explore mangrove lagoons—you'll get to see parts of the island that aren't accessible by road. It's a great activity for all skill levels, whether you're a first-timer or a seasoned kayaker. Many tours offer guided trips, which are perfect if you want to learn about the island's flora and fauna while paddling through crystal-clear waters.

Top Spots for Kayaking:
- <u>Marigot Bay</u>: Paddle through the calm, turquoise waters of this beautiful bay, surrounded by lush hills and charming waterfront bars. It's a peaceful and scenic spot, ideal for beginners.
- <u>Pigeon Island</u>: Kayak around the historic Pigeon Island National Park, exploring hidden coves and taking in views of Fort Rodney. It's a great way to combine a bit of history with your adventure.
- <u>Anse La Raye Mangroves:</u> If you're looking for something a bit different, join a guided tour through the mangroves near Anse La Raye. You'll paddle through narrow channels surrounded by dense vegetation, with plenty of opportunities for birdwatching.

- <u>Cost</u>: Kayak rentals typically cost around $20 - $30 USD per hour, while guided tours range from $50 - $75 USD per person.
- <u>What to Bring</u>: A hat, sunscreen, a waterproof phone case, and plenty of water.

<u>Pro Tip</u>: Early morning is the best time to kayak—there's less wind, the water is calmer, and you might spot more wildlife.

2. Paddleboarding

If you're looking for a fun and relaxing way to explore the water, give stand-up paddleboarding (SUP) a try. It's a fantastic way to get a full-body workout while enjoying the beautiful scenery. St. Lucia's calm bays and clear waters make it an ideal destination for paddleboarding. You can paddle along the coast, explore secluded beaches, or even try yoga on your board for a bit of extra challenge!

Top Spots for Paddleboarding:
- Reduit Beach: The calm waters here are perfect for paddleboarding, especially if you're a beginner. Rent a board from one of the beach vendors and glide along the shore, taking in the view of the vibrant Rodney Bay area.
- Marigot Bay: Paddle through this iconic bay, surrounded by yachts and the lush hills that make it one of the prettiest spots on the island. It's a peaceful, picturesque place for a relaxing paddle session.
- Sugar Beach: Located between the towering Pitons, this spot offers some of the best views in St. Lucia. Paddleboarding here feels like you're floating through a postcard!

- Cost: Board rentals start at around $20 USD per hour, while guided paddleboarding tours cost about $50 - $70 USD per person.

- **What to Bring:** Sunscreen, sunglasses with a strap, and a rash guard if you plan to spend a lot of time on the board.

Pro Tip: If you're new to paddleboarding, start out on your knees to get a feel for the balance before standing up. It's easier than it looks once you get the hang of it!

3. Jet Skiing

For those looking for a bit more adrenaline, jet skiing is the way to go. There's nothing quite like the thrill of speeding across the water with the wind in your hair. It's a fantastic way to explore the coastline quickly, and you'll have plenty of fun along the way. Most jet ski rentals in St. Lucia come with a quick safety briefing and are suitable for beginners and experienced riders alike.

Top Spots for Jet Skiing:
- **Rodney Bay:** This bustling area is a hotspot for jet skiing. You can rent a jet ski right from the beach and zip around the bay, enjoying the views of Reduit Beach and Pigeon Island.
- **Anse des Pitons (Sugar Beach):** Jet skiing between the iconic Pitons is an experience you'll never forget. The dramatic scenery and crystal-clear waters make it one of the most memorable places to ride.

- **Castries Harbor**: If you want a mix of urban and natural views, try jet skiing around the capital city's harbor. You'll get to see Castries from a unique perspective, zooming past the colorful waterfront and the iconic cathedral.

- **Cost**: Jet ski rentals typically range from $60 - $100 USD for a 30-minute session. Guided tours are available for around $150 USD per hour.
- **What to Bring**: Swimwear, a life jacket (provided by the rental company), and sunglasses.

Pro Tip: Follow the safety rules and listen to your instructor—jet skiing is fun but can be dangerous if you're not careful. Stick to the designated riding areas and keep an eye out for other watercraft.

Tips for Enjoying Water Sports in St. Lucia

- **Check the Weather:** Wind and waves can affect your experience, so try to plan your activities for a calm, sunny day. Early mornings often have the best conditions.
- **Stay Hydrated**: It's easy to get dehydrated out on the water, especially in the tropical heat. Bring a reusable water bottle and drink plenty of fluids.
- **Respect the Environment:** St. Lucia's waters are part of protected marine areas.

Be mindful of coral reefs, avoid disturbing marine life, and never leave trash behind.
- Book in Advance: During peak season (December to April), popular water sports activities can fill up quickly. Book your rentals or tours ahead of time to secure your spot.

How to Book Your Water Sports Adventure

You can rent equipment directly from beach vendors at popular spots like Reduit Beach and Marigot Bay, or book guided tours through local operators like Sea Spray Cruises or Aquaholics St. Lucia. Most hotels and resorts also offer water sports rentals and excursions, so check with your concierge for convenient options.

- Average Prices: Kayak rentals: $20 - $30 USD per hour, Paddleboard rentals: $20 USD per hour, Jet ski rentals: $60 - $100 USD per 30 minutes
- Best Tour Operators: Look for reputable companies with good reviews to ensure a safe and enjoyable experience. Popular choices include Dive Saint Lucia, Sea Spray Cruises, and Marigot Bay Water Sports.

C. Snorkeling and Scuba Diving

1. Anse Chastanet

If you're looking for the best spot to snorkel or dive in St. Lucia, Anse Chastanet should be at the top of your list. This beautiful beach near Soufrière is part of a protected marine reserve, which means the coral reefs are teeming with life. The waters are crystal clear, and you'll be surrounded by vibrant coral formations, schools of tropical fish, and even a few friendly turtles. It's a great spot for both snorkeling and scuba diving, with easy access right from the beach.

- Location: Near Soufrière, on the southwestern coast
- Entry Fee: Free public access (parking at the Anse Chastanet Resort may cost around $10 USD)
- What to See: Expect to spot parrotfish, trumpetfish, sergeant majors, and sometimes even rays gliding across the sandy bottom.

Snorkeling Tips: Head to the right side of the beach, where the coral reef starts just a few feet from the shore. Bring your own snorkeling gear if you have it, or rent from the dive shop on-site.

- Scuba Diving: Certified divers can explore deeper sections of the reef and even visit the famous Anse Chastanet Wall, which drops to about 150 feet (45 meters) and is covered in colorful sponges and corals.

Pro Tip: Book a night dive if you're feeling adventurous—the reef comes alive with nocturnal creatures like lobsters and octopuses!

2. Superman's Flight

For experienced divers looking for an adrenaline rush, the Superman's Flight Dive Site is a must-visit. Named after a scene from the Superman II movie that was filmed here, this dive is a thrilling drift along the base of Petit Piton, one of St. Lucia's iconic volcanic peaks. The current gently carries you along, making it an effortless yet exhilarating dive. The underwater landscape is dramatic, with steep walls covered in vibrant corals and sponges. Keep your eyes peeled for barracuda, moray eels, and even the occasional nurse shark.

- <u>Location</u>: Near Petit Piton, off the coast of Soufrière
- <u>Difficulty</u>: Advanced (drift diving experience recommended)
- <u>Depth:</u> Ranges from 40 to 120 feet (12 to 36 meters)
- <u>What to See:</u> Colorful corals, barrel sponges, large schools of fish, and sometimes bigger marine life like barracuda and sharks

<u>Pro Tip:</u> Bring an underwater camera—the visibility is usually excellent, and the dramatic underwater cliffs make for fantastic photos.

3. The Coral Gardens

If you're new to snorkeling or scuba diving, the Coral Gardens near Soufrière offer a fantastic introduction to St. Lucia's marine life. This spot is known for its shallow, gentle reefs that are perfect for beginners. The reef is home to a variety of soft and hard corals, and the calm waters make it an ideal spot for families and novice divers. You'll feel like you're swimming in an aquarium, surrounded by colorful fish and delicate sea fans swaying in the current.

- Location: Near Soufrière, within the Pitons Management Area
- Depth: Snorkelers will stay around 5-15 feet (1.5-4.5 meters), while divers can explore depths up to 60 feet (18 meters)
- What to See: You'll likely spot butterflyfish, angelfish, and vibrant coral formations. Keep an eye out for tiny critters like nudibranchs and cleaner shrimp hiding in the crevices.

Pro Tip: This spot gets popular in the afternoon with boat tours, so visit in the morning for a quieter experience.

4. The Wreck of the Lesleen M

For something a bit different, head to the Lesleen M, a sunken freighter that has become a vibrant artificial reef. This dive site is suitable for both beginners and experienced divers, offering depths ranging from 30 to 60 feet (9 to 18 meters). The wreck is covered in colorful corals and sponges, and it's home to a variety of marine life, including eels, crabs, and large schools of fish. Exploring the wreck is like taking a step back in time, as you swim through the remnants of the ship's structure.

- <u>Location:</u> Just off the coast of Anse Cochon
- <u>Difficulty</u>: Beginner to intermediate (ideal for wreck diving beginners)
- <u>What to See:</u> The wreck itself is impressive, with large open sections that are easy to swim through. Look for schools of snapper, moray eels hiding in the crevices, and sometimes even a sea turtle resting on the deck.

<u>Pro Tip:</u> Bring a dive light—it helps illuminate the interior of the wreck and reveals hidden marine life.

Tips for Snorkeling and Diving in St. Lucia

- <u>Check the Weather:</u> Calm, sunny days offer the best visibility for snorkeling and diving. If the water looks rough, ask a local guide for advice before heading out.
- <u>Bring Reef-Safe Sunscreen:</u> Help protect the delicate coral reefs by using a sunscreen that doesn't contain harmful chemicals.
- <u>Respect Marine Life:</u> Look, but don't touch! Corals and marine animals are fragile, and touching them can cause

damage. Enjoy the underwater world responsibly.
- Book a Guided Tour: Even if you're an experienced diver, booking a tour with a local dive shop like Scuba St. Lucia or Dive Saint Lucia can enhance your experience. The guides know the best spots and can point out things you might miss on your own.

How to Book Your Snorkeling or Diving Adventure

Most hotels and resorts offer snorkeling and diving excursions, or you can book directly with dive shops like Scuba St. Lucia, Dive Saint Lucia, and Action Adventure Divers. Prices for guided snorkeling tours start at around $40 - $60 USD per person, while diving trips typically range from $100 - $150 USD, including equipment.

- Average Prices: Snorkeling tours: $40 - $60 USD per person, Scuba diving: $100 - $150 USD per dive
- Top Dive Shops: Scuba St. Lucia, Dive Saint Lucia, Action Adventure Divers

Pro Tip: Book your excursions early, especially during the high season (December to April). Spots fill up fast, and you don't want to miss out!

D. Zip-Lining and Aerial Adventures: Soar Above St. Lucia's Rainforest Canopy

Hey there, adrenaline junkie! If you're looking for a thrill during your visit to St. Lucia, why not take to the skies? Let's dive into the best spots for zip-lining and aerial adventures on the island!

1. Rainforest Adventures St. Lucia

If you're looking for the most popular and comprehensive zip-lining experience on the island, head to Rainforest Adventures St. Lucia. Located in the Chassin area of Babonneau, this eco-park offers a series of thrilling zip lines that take you high above the rainforest floor. You'll zip from platform to platform, getting incredible views of the lush greenery and even catching glimpses of the island's wildlife. The highlight of the tour is the Adrena-Line, a heart-pounding ride that's one of the longest and fastest zip lines in St. Lucia.

- Location: Chassin, Babonneau (about a 30-minute drive from Castries)
- What's Included: A guided tour with trained instructors, 8 zip lines, and a suspension bridge walk through the jungle
- Cost: $90 - $100 USD per person (includes safety gear and instruction)
- Duration: About 2.5 hours for the full tour

- **What to Bring:** Wear comfortable clothes, closed-toe shoes, and don't forget your camera (just make sure it's secured—you don't want to drop it from the treetops!)

Pro Tip: Book your tour in advance, especially during the high season, as this is one of the most popular attractions on the island.

2. Treetop Adventure Park

For a zip-lining experience that's perfect for families and beginners, check out Treetop Adventure Park in the Dennery Valley. This park offers a variety of zip lines that cater to different comfort levels, making it a great choice for first-timers or those with younger kids. The zip lines here aren't as high or as fast as some of the others on the island, but they still offer plenty of excitement and beautiful views of the surrounding rainforest. The park is also home to the Longest and Fastest Zip Line in St. Lucia, stretching over 800 feet (244 meters)—an absolute must for thrill-seekers!

- **Location:** Dennery Valley, about a 40-minute drive from Castries
- **What's Included:** 12 zip lines, guided tour, and all safety equipment
- **Cost:** $70 - $85 USD per person, with discounts for kids
- **Duration:** About 2 hours

- **What to Bring:** Comfortable clothing, sturdy shoes, and bug spray (you're in the rainforest, after all!)

Pro Tip: This park also offers a Rainforest Hike and Waterfall Tour, so consider combining zip-lining with a trek through the jungle to see the beautiful Sault Falls.

3. Morne Coubaril Estate

If you want a zip-lining experience with a bit of history thrown in, head to Morne Coubaril Estate near Soufrière. This historic plantation offers a unique zip-lining tour that takes you over the estate's lush grounds, giving you a bird's-eye view of the cocoa and coffee fields below. The course features a series of short, exciting zip lines that crisscross the plantation, offering spectacular views of the Pitons and the surrounding jungle. It's a fantastic way to combine a bit of adventure with a cultural experience.

- **Location:** Near Soufrière, close to the Pitons
- **What's Included:** 8 zip lines, guided tour, and a visit to the plantation's historical exhibits (learn about St. Lucia's colonial history and traditional farming techniques)
- **Cost:** $60 - $75 USD per person (includes a tour of the estate)

- <u>Duration</u>: About 1.5 hours for the zip-lining tour, plus additional time for exploring the plantation
- <u>What to Bring</u>: Sunscreen, sunglasses, and a good sense of adventure

<u>Pro Tip:</u> After your zip-lining tour, stop by the plantation's restaurant to try some traditional St. Lucian dishes made with ingredients grown right on the estate.

4. Enbas Saut Rainforest Zip Line

For those looking for a more off-the-beaten-path zip-lining experience, the Enbas Saut Rainforest Zip Line offers a thrilling ride through the dense jungle of the Edmund Forest Reserve. This experience is less commercialized than some of the other options, making it ideal for those who want a more rustic, natural feel. The zip lines here are shorter but take you deep into the heart of the rainforest, where you can truly feel like you're flying through the jungle canopy.

- <u>Location</u>: Edmund Forest Reserve, near the Enbas Saut Waterfall Trail
- <u>What's Included</u>: 5 zip lines, guided tour, and a short hike through the rainforest
- <u>Cost</u>: $50 - $65 USD per person
- <u>Duration</u>: About 1.5 hours
- <u>What to Bring</u>: Hiking shoes, bug spray, and a rain jacket (the rainforest can get damp even on sunny days)

Pro Tip: Combine this experience with a hike to the nearby Enbas Saut Waterfall—it's one of the island's most beautiful and secluded falls.

Tips for Zip-Lining in St. Lucia

- Wear the Right Gear: Closed-toe shoes are a must, and comfortable, breathable clothing will make the experience more enjoyable.
- Check Weight Limits: Most zip-lining tours have weight limits (usually between 60 lbs and 275 lbs), so check with the tour operator before booking.
- Listen to Your Guide: The guides are trained to keep you safe and make sure you have a great time, so follow their instructions carefully.
- Don't Forget Your Camera: If you have a GoPro or a secure phone holder, bring it along. The views from the treetops are spectacular, and you'll want to capture the moment.
- Book in Advance: Zip-lining is a popular activity, especially during the high season (December to April). Booking ahead of time ensures you get the time slot you want.

How to Book Your Zip-Lining Adventure

You can book directly with the tour operators, such as Rainforest Adventures St. Lucia, Treetop

Adventure Park, or Morne Coubaril Estate, or through your hotel's concierge. Prices typically range from $50 - $100 USD per person, depending on the tour length and features. Many operators also offer combo packages that include other activities like hiking, waterfall tours, or plantation visits.

- <u>Average Prices:</u> $60 - $100 USD per person
- <u>Top Operators</u>: Rainforest Adventures St. Lucia, Treetop Adventure Park, Morne Coubaril Estate
- <u>Pro Tip:</u> Look for online discounts or book through your hotel for special rates or added perks like free transportation.

E. Whale Watching and Dolphin Tours

Hey there, nature enthusiast! If you've ever dreamed of seeing whales and dolphins in the wild, St. Lucia offers some of the best opportunities to do just that. Whether you're a seasoned wildlife watcher or a first-timer, these tours promise an unforgettable experience. Ready to set sail? Let's explore what you can expect on a whale watching and dolphin tour in St. Lucia!

1. The Best Time for Whale Watching in St. Lucia

St. Lucia's warm Caribbean waters are a prime spot for whale watching all year round, but the best time to catch a glimpse of these incredible creatures is during the winter and spring months (December to April). This period coincides with the migration patterns of several species of whales, making it the perfect time for sightings. You might see humpback whales, sperm whales, and even the elusive pilot whale. Dolphins are also abundant in these waters and can be seen throughout the year, with common species including the spinner dolphin, bottlenose dolphin, and the energetic Atlantic spotted dolphin.

- <u>Best Time to Go:</u> December to April (for whale sightings), year-round for dolphins
- <u>Pro Tip:</u> Morning tours tend to have calmer seas, which can make for a smoother ride and better visibility.

2. What to Expect on a Whale Watching Tour

A typical whale watching tour in St. Lucia lasts between 3 to 4 hours and takes you several miles offshore, where the waters are deep enough for whales. The tours are usually led by knowledgeable local guides who know the best spots to find these gentle giants. Most tours include a briefing session where you'll learn about the different species you might see and tips on how to spot them. As the boat cruises through the open sea, keep your eyes peeled for the telltale spout of a whale or the playful splash of a dolphin pod.

- Tour Duration: 3-4 hours
- Cost: $75 - $120 USD per person, depending on the tour operator and inclusions
- What's Included: Professional guide, refreshments (usually water and soft drinks), and sometimes snacks
- What to Bring: Sunglasses, sunscreen, a hat, and binoculars (if you have them)

Pro Tip: Sit at the front of the boat for the best views, but be prepared for a bit of splash—wear quick-drying clothes or bring a light rain jacket.

3. Top Operators for Whale Watching and Dolphin Tours

There are several reputable tour operators in St. Lucia that offer whale watching and dolphin tours. Here are a few of the best options:

Hackshaw's Boat Charters: One of the longest-running and most trusted operators in St. Lucia, Hackshaw's offers a 4-hour whale and dolphin watching tour that takes you out on a comfortable, stable catamaran. Their guides are experienced and have a great track record of sightings.

- Departure Point: Castries Harbor
- Cost: Around $90 USD per person

Pro Tip: Hackshaw's provides free drinks on board, including rum punch—perfect for toasting your first whale sighting!

Captain Mike's Whale Watching Tours: Captain Mike's is another excellent choice for a whale watching adventure. Their tours are led by experienced marine biologists who provide educational insights about the marine life you encounter. They also offer private charters for a more intimate experience.
- Departure Point: Rodney Bay Marina
- Cost: $100 - $120 USD per person

Pro Tip: Book a morning tour for the best chances of calm seas and optimal visibility.

Sea Spray Cruises: Known for their friendly guides and well-maintained boats, Sea Spray Cruises offers a combination tour that includes whale watching, snorkeling, and a coastal cruise. It's a great option if you want to pack multiple activities into one trip.
- Departure Point: Marigot Bay
- Cost: $110 USD per person

Pro Tip: Bring your snorkeling gear or rent it on board—Sea Spray often stops at a beautiful snorkeling spot after the whale watching tour.

4. Marine Life You Might Encounter

The waters around St. Lucia are rich with marine biodiversity. Here are some of the incredible creatures you might spot on your tour:

- <u>Humpback Whales:</u> Known for their acrobatic breaches and beautiful songs, humpback whales are a favorite among visitors. They're most commonly seen during their migration season from December to April.
- <u>Sperm Whales:</u> These deep-diving giants are known for their distinctive square-shaped heads. They're often spotted off the coast of St. Lucia, and seeing one in person is an awe-inspiring experience.
- <u>Pilot Whales:</u> These social whales are often seen traveling in large pods. They're smaller than humpbacks and sperm whales, but just as fascinating to watch.
- <u>Dolphins:</u> Spinner dolphins are famous for their playful behavior and spectacular jumps, while bottlenose dolphins are known for their friendly nature and love of swimming alongside boats.

<u>Pro Tip:</u> Keep your camera ready, but remember to put it down sometimes and just enjoy the moment—seeing these animals in the wild is truly magical.

Tips for a Great Whale Watching Experience

- <u>Bring Motion Sickness Medication:</u> Even if you don't usually get seasick, it's a good idea to take precautions. The sea can get choppy, especially in the afternoon.

- **Listen to Your Guide:** The guides are experts at spotting marine life, and they'll give you tips on where to look and what to watch for.
- **Be Patient:** Whale watching is all about timing and luck. You might not see a whale right away, but don't get discouraged—enjoy the ride and keep your eyes on the water.
- **Respect the Wildlife:** The tour operators follow strict guidelines to ensure the safety and well-being of the animals. Avoid loud noises and sudden movements, and never try to touch the marine life.

How to Book Your Tour

You can book a whale watching or dolphin tour through most hotels and resorts in St. Lucia, or directly with the tour operators. Online booking is also available through platforms like Viator and TripAdvisor, where you can read reviews and compare options. It's a good idea to book in advance, especially during peak season, as spots can fill up quickly.

- **Average Prices:** $75 - $120 USD per person
- **Top Operators:** Hackshaw's Boat Charters, Captain Mike's Whale Watching Tours, Sea Spray Cruises
- **Pro Tip:** Some operators offer a "no-sighting" guarantee, which means

you can join another tour for free if you don't see any whales or dolphins on your trip.

Chapter 9: Cultural Experiences

A. Festivals and Events in 2025

1. St. Lucia Independence Day (February 22nd)

St. Lucia's Independence Day is a celebration of national pride and cultural heritage. The island gained independence from Britain in 1979, and every year, St. Lucians come together to commemorate this important milestone. The festivities kick off with colorful parades, music, and dancing in the streets. The capital, Castries, is the heart of the celebration, where you can see traditional performances, enjoy local food stalls, and watch fireworks light up the sky.

- <u>Where to Go:</u> Head to Castries for the main events, including parades and concerts in Derek Walcott Square.

- **What to Expect:** Live music, traditional dance performances, and plenty of delicious street food like grilled fish and cassava bread.

Pro Tip: Get there early to snag a good viewing spot for the parade, and don't miss the cultural showcase in the evening, featuring local music and dance troupes.

2. St. Lucia Jazz and Arts Festival (May)

One of the island's most anticipated events, the St. Lucia Jazz and Arts Festival, is a must-see for music lovers. Held annually in May, this world-famous festival brings together local and international artists for a week of incredible performances. The main stage is set against the backdrop of the beautiful Pigeon Island National Park, where you can enjoy soulful jazz, reggae, and soca music while surrounded by stunning views of the Caribbean Sea.

- **Where to Go:** The main concerts take place at Pigeon Island National Park, but there are also events held in Castries and Rodney Bay.
- **What to Expect:** A mix of live music, art exhibitions, and fashion shows, plus plenty of food and drink stalls showcasing St. Lucia's best local cuisine.

Pro Tip: Book your tickets and accommodations early—this festival is extremely popular and tends to sell out fast. Don't forget your sunscreen and a hat for the daytime shows!

3. La Rose and La Marguerite Festivals (August and October)

For a deeper dive into St. Lucian culture, check out the La Rose (August 30th) and La Marguerite (October 17th) festivals. These two traditional flower festivals represent rival cultural societies on the island. The La Rose society is symbolized by the rose flower, while the La Marguerite society is represented by the marguerite flower. Each group holds lively parades, dances, and singing competitions, showcasing their unique traditions and costumes.

- Where to Go: Celebrations are held across the island, but the towns of Soufrière and Dennery are known for their vibrant parades and street parties.
- What to Expect: Colorful costumes, traditional folk songs, and dancing in the streets as each society tries to outdo the other in a friendly rivalry.

Pro Tip: Wear something red for La Rose and blue for La Marguerite to show your support for your chosen side. It's a fun way to immerse yourself in the festivities and feel like part of the community.

4. Carnival in St. Lucia (July)

St. Lucia's Carnival is one of the island's most exciting and energetic events, drawing visitors from around the world. Held in July, Carnival is a vibrant celebration of music, dance, and colorful costumes. The main events include the Calypso Monarch competition, the Panorama Steel Pan Competition, and the Parade of the Bands, where revelers dressed in dazzling costumes dance through the streets of Castries. It's a non-stop party, filled with the sounds of soca, calypso, and steel pan music.

- Where to Go: Castries is the center of the action, with the main parade route running through the city streets.
- What to Expect: High-energy street parties, incredible live music, and elaborate costumes that showcase the creativity and artistry of the island's designers.

Pro Tip: If you want to join in the fun, consider signing up with one of the local "mas bands" to get a costume and dance in the parade. It's a once-in-a-lifetime experience!

5. Jounen Kwéyòl (Creole Day, Last Sunday in October)

To experience the heart of St. Lucia's cultural heritage, don't miss Jounen Kwéyòl (Creole Day). Celebrated on the last Sunday in October, this island-wide festival honors the island's Creole roots with traditional music, dance, and food.

Towns and villages across St. Lucia host events where you can sample local dishes like bouyon, green fig and saltfish, and cocoa tea, while enjoying live performances of Creole folk music and storytelling.

- Where to Go: Celebrations are held all over the island, with different communities hosting the main events each year.
- What to Expect: A festive atmosphere with everyone dressed in traditional Creole attire, plenty of local food stalls, and cultural performances throughout the day.

Pro Tip: Try the local dishes and don't be shy about joining in the dancing—it's a great way to connect with locals and experience the island's warm, welcoming spirit.

B. Music, Dance, and Local Art

1. The Sounds of St. Lucia

St. Lucia's music scene is a lively mix of traditional sounds and modern influences, creating a vibrant soundtrack that reflects the island's cultural diversity. One of the most popular genres here is calypso, a style of music known for its witty lyrics and catchy melodies. Calypso songs often tell stories about island life, politics, and social issues, all with a humorous twist. You'll hear it everywhere during the Carnival season, when calypsonians compete for the title of Calypso Monarch.

- <u>Soca Music:</u> If you love to dance, soca music is your jam. This energetic genre evolved from calypso and is designed to get people moving with its fast beats and infectious rhythms. Soca songs are the life of the party during events like Carnival, where the crowds dance along to the lively tunes.
- <u>Dennery Segment</u>: A homegrown twist on soca music, Dennery Segment originated in the fishing village of Dennery. It's a high-energy, raw style of music that's taken the Caribbean by storm with its pounding beats and catchy lyrics. Expect to hear this unique sound at local parties and beach bars.

<u>Pro Tip:</u> Want to experience the music scene up close? Head to a local bar in Rodney Bay or Gros Islet on a Friday night for a live calypso or soca performance—you won't be able to sit still!

2. Dance

Dance is a huge part of St. Lucian culture, and it's a joyful way for locals to celebrate their heritage and traditions. Traditional dances like the quadrille date back to colonial times and are performed at cultural festivals and events. The quadrille is a lively, partner-based dance, similar to square dancing, and is often accompanied by Creole folk music.

- <u>Kwadril Dance:</u> This traditional folk dance has French roots and is performed in elegant attire, with dancers moving in intricate patterns. It's a dance that tells a story of community and togetherness, often performed during events like Jounen Kwéyòl (Creole Day).
- <u>Soca Dance:</u> At the other end of the spectrum, you've got the energetic moves of soca dancing. It's all about letting loose, feeling the rhythm, and having fun. You'll see soca dancers at street parties, Carnival events, and local festivals, moving to the fast-paced beats with infectious enthusiasm.

<u>Pro Tip:</u> Don't be shy if you're invited to dance! Locals love to teach visitors their moves, and it's a great way to join in the fun.

3. Local Art

St. Lucia's art scene is as vibrant as its music and dance, reflecting the island's natural beauty, cultural heritage, and daily life. You'll find local art everywhere—from galleries and studios to street markets and murals. The island's artists draw inspiration from the lush landscapes, colorful flora, and bustling local scenes, creating works that are rich in color and emotion.

- Visual Arts: St. Lucian painters and sculptors often use bright colors and bold shapes to capture the island's spirit. Visit the Eudovic Art Studio in Castries to see the incredible wood carvings made from local mahogany and cedar. These pieces often depict cultural figures, island wildlife, and abstract designs that tell stories about St. Lucian life.
- Castries Market: For a taste of local creativity, head to the Castries Market, where you can find paintings, handcrafted jewelry, and unique souvenirs made by local artisans. It's a great place to pick up a one-of-a-kind keepsake while supporting the island's creative community.

Pro Tip: Visit the Choiseul Arts and Craft Centre in the village of Choiseul for authentic local crafts like pottery, basket weaving, and hand-painted calabash bowls. It's a bit off the beaten path, but well worth the trip for the quality and variety of handmade items.

4. Live Performances

There's nothing quite like experiencing St. Lucia's music and dance live. The island is home to a variety of venues where you can catch performances ranging from traditional folk dances to modern soca and reggae shows. The Cultural Centre in Castries often hosts live performances, showcasing everything from

Creole folk music to contemporary St. Lucian bands.

- <u>Gros Islet Friday Night Street Party</u>: For an authentic local experience, head to the Gros Islet Friday Night Street Party, known as the Jump Up. It's a lively block party where the streets are filled with the sounds of calypso, soca, and reggae. You can dance, eat local street food, and enjoy the festive atmosphere alongside both locals and tourists.
- <u>Live Music at Pigeon Island:</u> During the St. Lucia Jazz and Arts Festival, Pigeon Island transforms into a massive outdoor venue, hosting some of the best live performances you'll see on the island. It's a mix of international jazz stars and local musicians, all set against the stunning backdrop of the Caribbean Sea.

<u>Pro Tip:</u> Check out the schedule at the Bay Gardens Beach Resort in Rodney Bay—they often host live music nights with local bands playing everything from reggae to calypso.

C. Exploring St. Lucian Cuisine

Ready to embark on a culinary journey? Let's explore some must-try dishes and food experiences in St. Lucia!

1. National Dish: Green Fig and Saltfish

Let's start with a classic—the national dish of St. Lucia, Green Fig and Saltfish. Despite its name, "green fig" refers to unripe bananas, which are boiled until tender and served with salted codfish that's sautéed with onions, tomatoes, garlic, and herbs. It's a hearty, flavorful dish that perfectly showcases the island's unique culinary traditions. You can find it served at local diners, food stalls, and even fancy restaurants, especially during special events and holidays.

- <u>Where to Try It:</u> Head to the Castries Market in the morning for an authentic plate of Green Fig and Saltfish. It's a popular breakfast dish among locals, so you'll get a taste of traditional St. Lucian morning fare.

<u>Pro Tip</u>: Pair it with a cup of cocoa tea, a traditional hot chocolate drink made with local cocoa, spices, and milk. It's rich, comforting, and a perfect complement to the dish.

2. Creole-Style Seafood

St. Lucia's location in the Caribbean means seafood is a staple of the local diet. You'll find fresh fish, shrimp, crab, and lobster on menus across the island, often prepared with a Creole twist. Creole-style seafood dishes are typically seasoned with a blend of local spices and cooked with onions, tomatoes, peppers, and herbs, creating a vibrant, flavorful experience.

- <u>Must-Try Dish:</u> Order the Creole fish stew, a spicy, savory dish made with fresh catch-of-the-day fish simmered in a rich tomato-based sauce. It's usually served with rice, plantains, or breadfruit.
- <u>Where to Eat</u>: For an authentic experience, visit a seaside restaurant like The Naked Fisherman in Cap Estate or Martha's Table in Soufrière. These spots offer stunning views and dishes made with the freshest local seafood.

<u>Pro Tip:</u> Try the spiny lobster if you're visiting during lobster season (August to February). It's a local delicacy often grilled and served with garlic butter.

3. Street Food

If you want to experience St. Lucian cuisine like a local, don't miss the chance to try the island's street food. The streets come alive with vendors offering a variety of tasty snacks and quick bites that are perfect for an afternoon treat or a late-night munch. You'll find everything from fried bakes (a type of savory doughnut) filled with saltfish to roti, a Caribbean flatbread stuffed with curried meat or vegetables.

- <u>Must-Try Snack:</u> Accra, a popular street food made of deep-fried fish fritters.

These crispy, savory bites are made with salted cod and a mix of herbs and spices, then fried to golden perfection. They're often sold in small paper bags, making them a great grab-and-go snack.
- <u>Where to Find It:</u> Check out the Gros Islet Friday Night Street Party (Jump Up) or the Castries Market for the best street food options. It's a lively scene with plenty of vendors cooking up delicious eats right before your eyes.

<u>Pro Tip:</u> Try a local juice like tamarind or passion fruit to wash down your street food. These refreshing drinks are made with fresh island fruits and offer a sweet, tangy taste of St. Lucia.

4. Sweet Treats

Got a sweet tooth? You're in luck, because St. Lucia has some incredible desserts that showcase the island's tropical fruits and local flavors. One must-try is coconut cake, a moist, fluffy cake made with freshly grated coconut and a hint of nutmeg. Another favorite is cassava pone, a chewy, dense cake made with grated cassava, coconut, spices, and sometimes raisins.

- <u>Where to Indulge:</u> Stop by a local bakery or the Castries Market for fresh coconut cakes and cassava pone. Many restaurants also offer these treats on their dessert menus.

Pro Tip: If you visit during the Jounen Kwéyòl (Creole Day) celebrations, you'll find a wide array of traditional desserts, including sugar cakes (coconut candy) and banana fritters.

5. Rum: The Spirit of St. Lucia

No culinary journey in St. Lucia is complete without sampling the island's famous rum. St. Lucian rum is known for its bold, rich flavor, and you'll find it featured in cocktails at bars and restaurants across the island. One of the best ways to experience the local rum culture is by visiting a distillery, where you can learn about the production process and sample different varieties.

- Where to Go: Visit the St. Lucia Distillers in Roseau Valley for a guided tour and tasting session. You'll get to try a range of rums, from the smooth Chairman's Reserve to the sweet, spiced Bounty Rum.
- Must-Try Cocktail: Order a Piton Punch, made with local rum, pineapple juice, grenadine, and lime. It's a refreshing, fruity drink that's perfect for sipping by the beach.

Pro Tip: Pick up a bottle of Chairman's Reserve to bring home as a souvenir—it's one of the island's best-loved rums and makes a great gift for friends or family.

D. Museums and Historical Sites

1. Pigeon Island National Park

One of the most popular historical attractions in St. Lucia is Pigeon Island National Park, a beautiful 44-acre reserve that's packed with history and stunning views. Once a strategic military outpost, Pigeon Island has a rich past involving battles between the French and British for control of the Caribbean. Today, you can explore the ruins of Fort Rodney, a British fort built in the late 18th century. Hike up to the fort for incredible panoramic views of the island and the turquoise waters below.

- <u>Location</u>: Near Gros Islet, accessible via a causeway
- <u>Entry Fee</u>: $10 USD per person
- <u>What to See:</u> The ruins of Fort Rodney, old cannons, and the historic barracks. There's also a small museum where you can learn about the island's colonial history.

<u>Pro Tip:</u> Bring your camera for the breathtaking views from the top of Fort Rodney, and don't miss the beach at Pigeon Island—it's a great spot for a swim after exploring the historical sites.

2. The Morne Coubaril Estate

For a hands-on history experience, visit Morne Coubaril Estate near Soufrière. This working plantation dates back to the 18th century and offers guided tours that take you through the estate's historic grounds. You'll see traditional methods of producing cocoa, coffee, and coconut products, and even get to sample some of the estate's fresh-made treats. The tour includes a visit to a replica of a traditional St. Lucian village, giving you a feel for what life was like on the island centuries ago.

- Location: Soufrière, near the Pitons
- Entry Fee: $30 - $40 USD per person (includes guided tour and tastings)
- What to See: The traditional cocoa-raking process, the old sugar mill, and the replica village. You can also try zip-lining over the plantation for an added thrill!

Pro Tip: Don't leave without tasting the fresh cocoa tea made on-site—it's a rich, chocolatey drink that's a true taste of St. Lucia.

3. The St. Lucia National Archives and Folk Research Centre

If you're interested in learning about the island's Creole heritage, the St. Lucia National Archives and Folk Research Centre in Castries is a must-visit. This center is dedicated to preserving the island's cultural history, with exhibits that highlight the traditional music, dance, language, and customs of St. Lucia's Creole people. It's a great place to explore if you want to understand more about the island's unique blend of African, European, and Indigenous influences.

- Location: Castries, near Derek Walcott Square
- Entry Fee: Free, though donations are appreciated
- What to See: Exhibits on St. Lucia's folk traditions, including Kwéyòl language materials, traditional clothing, and musical instruments like the banjo and quatro.

Pro Tip: Visit during Jounen Kwéyòl (Creole Day) in October for special events, including live music, dance performances, and Creole cooking demonstrations.

4. La Toc Battery

For a more off-the-beaten-path experience, check out the La Toc Battery, a lesser-known historical site that offers a fascinating look into St. Lucia's military past. Built in the late 19th century by the British, this coastal fort was part of the island's defense system during the colonial era. Today, you can explore the old gun emplacements and underground tunnels, which were used to store ammunition. The site also offers stunning views of the Castries harbor.

- Location: Near La Toc Beach, Castries
- Entry Fee: Free (self-guided tours)

- **What to See:** The old cannons, underground tunnels, and lookout points. It's a quiet spot with a lot of history, perfect for those who enjoy exploring on their own.

Pro Tip: Wear sturdy shoes—the path to the battery can be a bit uneven, but the views and the history make it well worth the effort.

5. The Eudovic Art Studio and Museum

For a unique blend of history and art, visit the Eudovic Art Studio and Museum. This family-run studio in Castries is home to some of St. Lucia's finest wood carvings, created by master sculptor Vincent Joseph Eudovic and his family. The museum features a collection of traditional and contemporary wood sculptures that reflect the island's culture and history. It's a great place to learn about the craftsmanship behind St. Lucia's art scene and pick up a one-of-a-kind souvenir.

- Location: Castries, near Morne Fortune
- Entry Fee: Free (guided tours available for a small fee)
- What to See: The gallery of intricate wood carvings, workshops where you can see the artists at work, and the outdoor sculpture garden.
- Pro Tip: Take a guided tour to learn about the symbolism behind the sculptures. The Eudovic family is happy to share stories

about their art and the cultural influences that inspire their work.

Tips for Visiting Museums and Historical Sites in St. Lucia

- Bring Cash: Some of the smaller sites and museums don't accept credit cards, so it's a good idea to have cash on hand for entry fees and souvenirs.
- Plan for Extra Time: Many of these sites have beautiful grounds and surrounding areas to explore, so don't rush through your visit. Take your time to soak in the history and scenery.
- Ask Questions: The guides and staff at these sites are often passionate about their island's history and culture. Don't be shy about asking questions—they love sharing their knowledge and stories.

Chapter 10: St. Lucian Food and Drink

A. Must-Try Dishes and Street Food

Let's dive into some of the must-try dishes and street food you can't miss while visiting St. Lucia!

1. Green Fig and Saltfish

Let's kick things off with a classic—Green Fig and Saltfish, the national dish of St. Lucia. Despite the name, "green fig" refers to unripe bananas, which are boiled until tender and mixed with salted codfish sautéed with onions, tomatoes, garlic, and local herbs. This hearty and flavorful dish is a staple in St. Lucian households and a must-try for any visitor looking to experience authentic island cuisine.

- <u>Where to Try It:</u> Head to the Castries Market in the morning for a fresh, homemade plate of Green Fig and Saltfish. It's often served for breakfast, so it's a great way to start your day like a local.

Pro Tip: Pair it with a cup of traditional cocoa tea, a spiced hot chocolate made with locally grown cocoa. It's rich, comforting, and the perfect complement to the dish.

2. Bouyon

If you're looking for a comforting meal, try bouyon, a thick, flavorful stew that's a favorite on the island. Made with a mix of meats (usually chicken, pork, or fish), root vegetables, dumplings, and local spices, bouyon is a hearty dish that's perfect for a satisfying lunch or dinner. It's often cooked slowly to allow the flavors to blend, resulting in a savory, filling meal that's packed with flavor.

- Where to Eat: You can find bouyon at many local diners and food stalls, especially on Fridays when it's traditionally served. Check out Martha's Table in Soufrière for a delicious, home-cooked version.

Pro Tip: Don't be shy about asking for extra dumplings—they're one of the best parts of the dish!

3. Accra

For a tasty snack on the go, grab some accra, also known as codfish fritters. These bite-sized treats are made by mixing salted codfish with flour, spices, and herbs, then deep-frying them until golden brown and crispy. They're a popular street food item and make for a perfect snack while exploring the island.

- <u>Where to Find It:</u> Accra is a common find at street vendors and local markets like the Gros Islet Friday Night Street Party (Jump Up). It's a must-try if you want to experience the flavors of St. Lucia's street food scene.

<u>Pro Tip</u>: Enjoy your accra with a side of pepper sauce for an extra kick of heat!

4. Roti

Roti is a beloved dish throughout the Caribbean, and St. Lucia is no exception. It's a warm, flaky flatbread stuffed with a savory filling, usually curried chicken, beef, or vegetables. The curry is rich and flavorful, spiced with turmeric, cumin, and local herbs, and the roti itself is soft and satisfying. It's a filling, grab-and-go meal that's perfect for lunch or a quick bite while sightseeing.

- <u>Where to Eat:</u> Try a roti from a local favorite like The Lime in Rodney Bay. Their chicken and vegetable roti are highly recommended and made fresh to order.

Pro Tip: Be prepared to get your hands a little messy—roti is best enjoyed without utensils. Just unwrap it and dive in!

5. Breadfruit and Fish Cakes

If you want a taste of something truly local, order breadfruit and fish cakes. Breadfruit is a starchy, potato-like fruit that's boiled or roasted and served with crispy fish cakes made from salted cod. The breadfruit has a mild, slightly nutty flavor that pairs perfectly with the savory, fried fish cakes. It's a simple yet delicious dish that's a staple at family gatherings and local events.

- Where to Try It: Check out local food stalls in Soufrière or Vieux Fort for an authentic plate of breadfruit and fish cakes. It's a popular choice during the weekend, especially at beachside shacks.

Pro Tip: Ask for some green seasoning on the side—it's a local condiment made from a blend of herbs and spices that adds an extra burst of flavor.

6. Sweet Treats

St. Lucia isn't just about savory dishes—the island's desserts are just as tasty and showcase the region's tropical ingredients. One must-try is coconut cake, a moist, fluffy cake made with freshly grated coconut and flavored with nutmeg and cinnamon. Another popular dessert is cassava pone, a chewy, dense cake made from grated cassava, coconut, and spices. It's sweet, slightly sticky, and full of flavor.

- Where to Indulge: Pick up a slice of coconut cake or cassava pone at the Castries Market or a local bakery. It's a great treat to enjoy with a cup of hot cocoa or coffee.

Pro Tip: If you're visiting during a local festival like Jounen Kwéyòl (Creole Day), you'll find an even wider selection of traditional sweets and snacks to try.

Tips for Enjoying St. Lucian Street Food

- Bring Cash: Many street food vendors only accept cash, so it's a good idea to have small bills on hand.
- Try New Things: Don't be afraid to sample dishes you've never heard of before—the locals take pride in their cuisine, and trying something new is part of the adventure.
- Watch for Spice: St. Lucian food can be spicy, especially when it comes to sauces and marinades. If you're sensitive to heat, ask for your dish without extra pepper sauce.

B. Top Restaurants and Cafés

Let's show you the top restaurants and cafés you won't want to miss, complete with their locations, best times to visit, prices, and insider tips. Get ready to discover St. Lucia's most delicious spots!

1. The Naked Fisherman Beach Bar & Grill

- Location: Cap Estate, nestled on the beachfront of Smuggler's Cove
- When to Visit: Open daily from 11 AM to 10 PM; best visited during sunset for the stunning views
- Price Range: Main dishes range from $25 - $45 USD
- What to Try: The grilled lobster and conch fritters are local favorites. Don't miss the tropical rum punch, a house specialty.

- Details: The Naked Fisherman offers a relaxed, beachside vibe with tables right on the sand. It's perfect for a romantic dinner or a casual lunch with friends. The menu focuses on fresh seafood, and the atmosphere is friendly and welcoming. The view of the ocean at sunset is unforgettable, so arrive early to secure a good spot.

Pro Tip: Make a reservation if you plan to visit for dinner, especially during the high season (December to April). Parking is limited, so consider taking a taxi from your hotel.

2. Dasheene at Ladera Resort

- Location: Soufrière, at the Ladera Resort overlooking the Pitons
- When to Visit: Open daily from 7 AM to 10 PM; visit for lunch (11 AM - 3 PM) or dinner (5 PM - 10 PM) for the best views of the Pitons
- Price Range: Lunch mains start at $35 USD, dinner entrees range from $45 - $70 USD
- What to Try: The coconut-crusted shrimp is a standout appetizer. For your main course, try the Pitons Catch of the Day. End your meal with the banana flambé, prepared tableside.
- Details: Dasheene is one of St. Lucia's top fine dining spots, offering breathtaking views of the Pitons. The open-air restaurant focuses on farm-to-table dining, using fresh, local ingredients in every dish. It's an ideal choice for a romantic night out or a special occasion meal.

Pro Tip: Reserve a table in advance and request a seat by the edge for the best panoramic views.

Dress code is smart casual, so leave the flip-flops behind.

3. Martha's Table

- Location: Soufrière, nestled in the hills near the Diamond Falls Botanical Gardens
- When to Visit: Open Monday to Saturday, 11 AM - 8 PM; best for lunch after a morning exploring Soufrière
- Price Range: Most dishes range from $15 - $25 USD
- What to Try: The stewed chicken with rice and peas is a must-try, as well as the coconut curry fish.
- Details: Martha's Table offers an authentic taste of St. Lucian home cooking. The restaurant is family-run, and you'll often find Martha herself in the kitchen. The menu features hearty, traditional dishes made with love, using fresh, locally sourced ingredients.

Pro Tip: Call ahead to find out the daily specials—Martha's Table often features seasonal dishes made with local produce. It's cash-only, so bring some EC dollars or USD.

4. Orlando's Restaurant & Bar

- Location: Soufrière, near the waterfront on Bridge Street

- **When to Visit:** Open Wednesday to Monday, 5 PM - 10 PM; ideal for dinner
- **Price Range:** Dinner entrees range from $30 - $60 USD
- **What to Try:** Opt for the tasting menu for a diverse selection of local flavors. The spiced mahi-mahi and the coconut shrimp soup are crowd favorites.
- **Details**: Orlando's offers a mix of Creole and Caribbean cuisine with a gourmet twist. Chef Orlando is passionate about using local ingredients, and his creativity shines through in every dish. The restaurant has a cozy, intimate atmosphere, perfect for a relaxed dining experience.

Pro Tip: The tasting menu changes regularly, so you'll get a unique experience every time you visit. Book a table in advance, as the restaurant is small and fills up quickly.

5. Big Yard Café & Bar

- **Location**: Gros Islet, at the heart of the Gros Islet Friday Night Street Party
- **When to Visit:** Open Thursday to Sunday, 12 PM - 11 PM; visit on Friday night for the street party atmosphere
- **Price Range**: Affordable, with most dishes under $15 USD

- <u>What to Try</u>: The jerk chicken and fish roti are must-haves. Pair it with a cold Pitons beer.

- <u>Details</u>: Big Yard Café & Bar is a lively, local spot known for its delicious street food and vibrant atmosphere. It's the perfect place to sample classic St. Lucian dishes while enjoying live music and the energy of the Gros Islet street party.

<u>Pro Tip</u>: Bring cash, as most vendors and small spots like Big Yard prefer cash payments. Arrive early to grab a seat before the party gets into full swing.

C. Best Local Bars and Nightlife

Let's explore some of the best places to drink, dance, and soak up the island vibes.

1. The Rum Cave

- <u>Location</u>: Marigot Bay Resort, Marigot Bay
- <u>When to Visit:</u> Open daily from 4 PM to midnight; visit around sunset for a relaxed start to your evening
- <u>Price Range:</u> Cocktails range from $12 - $20 USD
- <u>What to Try:</u> Start with a classic Rum Punch, then sample the Chairman's

Reserve rum flight for a taste of the island's best local rums.

- Details: The Rum Cave is a cozy, intimate bar located in Marigot Bay Resort, offering a sophisticated yet laid-back atmosphere. With a focus on locally produced rums, the bar features a wide selection of St. Lucian rums and creative cocktails. The decor is rustic, with wooden barrels and comfortable seating that give it a warm, inviting feel. It's a great place to unwind, learn about the island's rum-making traditions, and chat with the friendly bartenders.

Pro Tip: Ask for a rum tasting session—you'll get a guided tour of the different varieties, including the island's famous Bounty Rum. It's a great way to kick off your night with some local flavor.

2. Gros Islet Street Party (Jump Up)

- Location: Gros Islet, near Rodney Bay
- When to Visit: Every Friday night from 7 PM until late (often past midnight)
- Price Range: Drinks start at $5 USD, with food items ranging from $5 - $15 USD
- What to Try: Grab a cold Pitons beer or try a locally made spiced rum drink. Pair it with jerk chicken or fresh grilled fish from one of the street vendors.

- **Details**: The Gros Islet Street Party, also known as Jump Up, is the biggest weekly event on the island and a must-do for any visitor looking to experience local nightlife. The streets of Gros Islet come alive with music, dancing, and food stalls, creating a festive, carnival-like atmosphere. It's a great place to mingle with locals, enjoy live calypso and reggae music, and sample delicious street food.

Pro Tip: Arrive early to explore the food stalls before the crowd builds up. Bring cash, as most vendors don't accept cards. The vibe is very casual, so dress comfortably and get ready to dance the night away!

3. The Landings Beach Club

- **Location**: The Landings Resort & Spa, Rodney Bay
- **When to Visit:** Open daily from 11 AM to midnight; best visited in the evening for cocktails by the beach
- **Price Range:** Cocktails range from $15 - $25 USD
- **What to Try**: Sip on the St. Lucian Mojito, made with fresh local mint and premium St. Lucian rum. For something unique, try the Chocolate Martini, crafted with local cocoa.

- <u>Details</u>: If you're looking for a more upscale nightlife experience, The Landings Beach Club offers a chic, beachfront setting with fantastic views of Rodney Bay. The bar serves a variety of craft cocktails, local and international wines, and small plates featuring fresh, locally sourced ingredients. It's the perfect spot for a romantic date night or a relaxed evening with friends.

- <u>Pro Tip</u>: Time your visit for the live music nights, usually held on Fridays and Saturdays. The smooth jazz and acoustic performances create a mellow vibe that's perfect for unwinding.

4. Spice of India

- <u>Location</u>: Baywalk Mall, Rodney Bay
- <u>When to Visit:</u> Open daily from 5 PM to 11 PM; happy hour specials from 5 PM to 7 PM
- <u>Price Range:</u> Cocktails and craft drinks range from $10 - $18 USD
- <u>What to Try:</u> Their signature cocktail, the Spiced Rum Martini, is a must-try. If you're feeling adventurous, order the Coconut Cooler, a tropical twist on a classic mojito.
- <u>Details</u>: Spice of India isn't just known for its fantastic food—it's also home to one of

the best cocktail lounges on the island. The bar menu features an array of creative cocktails that blend local ingredients with Indian-inspired flavors. The ambiance is chic yet welcoming, making it a great spot for pre-dinner drinks or a nightcap.

Pro Tip: Arrive during happy hour for the best deals on cocktails and small plates. The bartenders are friendly and love to chat about the unique ingredients they use, so don't hesitate to ask for recommendations.

5. Delirius

- Location: Rodney Bay Village
- When to Visit: Open Tuesday to Sunday, 4 PM to 2 AM; best visited on weekends for the liveliest crowd
- Price Range: Cocktails range from $10 - $15 USD, beers start at $5 USD
- What to Try: Try the Passion Fruit Daiquiri or the popular Mango Margarita. For a local flavor, ask for the Creole Rum Punch.

- Details: Delirius is one of Rodney Bay's most popular bars, known for its vibrant atmosphere and creative cocktail menu. The bar has a large outdoor patio that's perfect for socializing, and the upbeat music sets the tone for a fun night out. It's a favorite spot among both locals and tourists, especially on weekends when the dance floor fills up with party-goers.

Pro Tip: Check their event schedule before you go—Delirius often hosts live DJ nights, themed parties, and cocktail-making classes.

Tips for Enjoying St. Lucia's Nightlife

- Bring Cash: Many bars, especially at street parties, prefer cash payments. ATMs can be scarce late at night, so plan ahead.
- Safety First: Stick to well-lit, busy areas, especially if you're exploring after dark. It's best to travel in a group or take a taxi back to your hotel.
- Try the Local Rum: St. Lucia is famous for its rum, so make sure to sample some local varieties like Chairman's Reserve or Bounty Rum.

200

Chapter 11: Shopping and Souvenirs

A. Local Markets and Artisan Shops

Hey there, shopper! If you're looking for unique, authentic souvenirs and local treasures to take home, you've come to the right place. Ready to explore? Let's dive into the best spots for finding those special St. Lucian keepsakes.

1. Castries Market

<u>Location</u>: Central Castries, near Derek Walcott Square
<u>When to Visit</u>: Open Monday to Saturday, 7 AM - 4 PM; best visited in the morning for the freshest produce and best selection
<u>What to Expect</u>: Castries Market is the largest and most famous market on the island, offering a vibrant mix of local crafts, fresh produce, spices, and street food. The market is bustling with activity, and it's a great place to find unique souvenirs like hand-painted calabash bowls, woven baskets, and colorful island fabrics.

<u>Must-Buy Items:</u>
- <u>Spices</u>: Stock up on fresh cinnamon, nutmeg, and allspice—perfect for adding a touch of the Caribbean to your cooking back home.

- **Handmade Crafts:** Look for straw hats, woven bags, and wooden carvings made by local artisans.
- **Local Delicacies:** Don't leave without trying a sample of the island's famous cocoa sticks (used for making traditional cocoa tea) or grabbing a jar of St. Lucian hot pepper sauce.

Pro Tip: Bring cash and small bills, as most vendors don't accept credit cards. It's also a good idea to wear comfortable shoes since you'll be doing a lot of walking. If you want a quieter experience, visit early in the morning before the crowds arrive.

2. Choiseul Arts and Craft Centre

Location: Choiseul Village, on the southwestern coast of the island
When to Visit: Open Monday to Saturday, 9 AM - 5 PM
What to Expect: The Choiseul Arts and Craft Centre is a hidden gem, known for its beautiful handmade crafts created by local artisans. This small, community-run shop specializes in traditional crafts like pottery, woven baskets, and intricate wood carvings. It's the perfect place to find a unique, locally made gift that tells a story of St. Lucian culture and craftsmanship.

Must-Buy Items:

- <u>Pottery</u>: Look for handcrafted clay pots and vases, often decorated with traditional island motifs.
- <u>Baskets</u>: The woven baskets here are made from locally sourced materials and come in various sizes and patterns—great for storage or as decorative pieces.
- <u>Wood Carvings:</u> The detailed wood sculptures, often depicting local wildlife or cultural symbols, make for stunning souvenirs.
- <u>Pro Tip:</u> Strike up a conversation with the artisans—they're friendly and love to share the history behind their crafts. It's a great way to learn more about the cultural significance of your purchase.

3. Eudovic's Art Studio

<u>Location</u>: Goodlands, near Castries
<u>When to Visit:</u> Open Monday to Friday, 9 AM - 4 PM; Saturday by appointment only
<u>What to Expect:</u> Eudovic's Art Studio is a must-visit for anyone interested in local art. Run by master sculptor Vincent Joseph Eudovic and his family, this studio showcases some of the finest wood carvings on the island. Each piece is crafted from local mahogany, cedar, or teak wood, and the designs often reflect St. Lucian culture, history, and nature. You'll find everything from small figurines to large, intricate sculptures.

Must-Buy Items:
- Figurines: Small wooden figurines are perfect for a unique souvenir that doesn't take up much space in your luggage.
- Abstract Carvings: Eudovic's signature abstract designs make for striking home decor pieces and conversation starters.
- Custom Pieces: If you're looking for something truly special, ask about commissioning a custom carving—perfect for a memorable gift.

Pro Tip: Take the guided tour of the studio to see the artists at work. It's fascinating to watch the carving process and learn about the techniques used. Be sure to bring your camera, as the sculptures are incredibly photogenic.

4. Anse La Raye Arts and Crafts Village

Location: Anse La Raye Village, along the west coast

When to Visit: Open daily, but weekends are best for local craft markets and live music

What to Expect: This small artisan village offers a more intimate shopping experience, with local vendors selling handmade crafts, jewelry, and paintings. The village is known for its vibrant arts scene, and you'll often find artists working on their creations right at their stalls. It's a great spot to pick up locally made jewelry, beachwear, and unique artwork while enjoying the laid-back vibe of the village.

Must-Buy Items:
- Jewelry: Look for handcrafted pieces made from local materials like seashells, coconut, and coral.
- Beachwear: Pick up a colorful sarong or beach wrap made from island-inspired fabrics.
- Paintings: Local artists often sell small, framed paintings depicting St. Lucian landscapes and everyday life scenes.

Pro Tip: Visit on a Friday evening for the Fish Fry, a popular local event where you can enjoy fresh seafood, music, and a festive atmosphere. It's a great way to end a day of shopping and exploring.

Tips for Shopping at Local Markets and Artisan Shops

- Bargain Respectfully: It's common to negotiate prices at markets, but always do so with respect. Offer a fair counteroffer rather than lowballing.
- Look for Authentic Goods: To ensure you're buying genuine local crafts, ask the vendor about the origin of the item. Avoid mass-produced souvenirs that are often imported.

- <u>Bring Cash:</u> Most markets and small shops don't accept credit cards, so it's best to carry cash in small denominations.
- <u>Ask for a Story:</u> Many items have cultural significance or are tied to local traditions. Don't hesitate to ask the seller about the story behind your purchase—it makes the souvenir even more meaningful.

B. Best Places to Buy Souvenirs

1. Castries Market

<u>Location</u>: Central Castries, near the harbor and Derek Walcott Square
<u>When to Visit:</u> Open Monday to Saturday, 7 AM - 4 PM; best visited in the morning for the freshest finds
<u>What to Expect:</u> This bustling market is the go-to spot for both locals and tourists. It's filled with vendors selling everything from fresh spices and local snacks to handmade crafts and traditional St. Lucian clothing. The vibrant atmosphere and friendly vendors make it a fun place to shop and explore.

<u>Top Souvenirs to Buy:</u>
- <u>Spices</u>: Pick up packets of cinnamon, nutmeg, and bay leaves—perfect for recreating Caribbean flavors at home.

- <u>Local Art:</u> Look for small paintings and handcrafted jewelry made from shells, beads, and local stones.
- <u>Handmade Baskets and Bags:</u> The market has a great selection of woven baskets and bags, ideal for gifts or practical souvenirs.

<u>Pro Tip:</u> Bring cash (preferably small bills) and don't be afraid to haggle a bit—it's part of the shopping experience. Aim to arrive early to beat the crowds and get first dibs on the best items.

2. The Baywalk Mall

<u>Location</u>: Rodney Bay, Gros Islet
<u>When to Visit:</u> Open daily from 9 AM to 8 PM; great for afternoon shopping or evening browsing
<u>What to Expect</u>: The Baywalk Mall offers a mix of high-end stores, local boutiques, and souvenir shops. It's a great place to find a variety of items, from designer beachwear and jewelry to locally made crafts. You'll also find duty-free shops, making it a great spot to pick up luxury goods at lower prices.

<u>Top Souvenirs to Buy:</u>
- <u>Local Rum:</u> Head to one of the duty-free liquor stores and pick up a bottle of Chairman's Reserve or Bounty Rum, two of St. Lucia's most famous spirits.

- **Beauty Products:** Look for natural, island-inspired skincare products made with local ingredients like coconut oil and cocoa butter.
- **Jewelry:** The mall has several shops selling beautiful, handcrafted pieces featuring local gemstones and seashells.

- **Pro Tip:** Take advantage of the mall's duty-free pricing, especially if you're buying rum or high-end items. Remember to bring your passport for duty-free purchases.

3. Choiseul Craft Market

Location: Choiseul Village, on the southwestern coast

When to Visit: Open Monday to Saturday, 9 AM - 5 PM; weekends are the best time to visit for a full selection of crafts

What to Expect: The Choiseul Craft Market is a must-visit for those seeking authentic, handmade souvenirs. The market showcases the work of local artisans who specialize in traditional crafts like pottery, basket weaving, and wood carving. It's a quieter, more relaxed shopping experience compared to the Castries Market, and you'll find unique items that reflect the island's cultural heritage.

Top Souvenirs to Buy:

- **Pottery and Ceramics:** Look for hand-painted vases and dishes that feature traditional St. Lucian designs.
- **Woven Items:** The baskets and hats here are made from locally sourced materials and crafted by hand—perfect for a unique gift.
- **Wood Carvings:** These beautifully detailed pieces often depict local wildlife or cultural symbols and make great decorative items for your home.

Pro Tip: Take your time browsing and chatting with the artisans. They love to share the stories behind their work, making your souvenir even more special. Bring cash, as most vendors don't accept cards.

4. Pink Plantation House

Location: Castries, set in the lush hills overlooking the city
When to Visit: Open Tuesday to Saturday, 10 AM - 4 PM; make it a lunch stop and enjoy the stunning views
What to Expect: The Pink Plantation House is a beautiful, historic estate that doubles as an art gallery and gift shop. It's a fantastic place to find unique, handcrafted souvenirs while enjoying a bit of history and stunning views of Castries. The gift shop features local pottery, hand-painted ceramics, and artwork created by St. Lucian artists.

Top Souvenirs to Buy:
- Ceramics: The hand-painted pottery is a highlight, with vibrant designs inspired by the island's flora and fauna.
- Local Artwork: You'll find a variety of paintings and prints depicting St. Lucian landscapes and everyday life scenes.
- Home Décor: Pick up colorful cushions, placemats, and other textiles featuring Caribbean-inspired patterns.

Pro Tip: Plan your visit around lunchtime and enjoy a meal at the estate's restaurant. The food is locally sourced and delicious, and the terrace offers breathtaking views of the city and coastline.

5. Anse Chastanet Gift Shop

Location: Anse Chastanet Resort, Soufrière
When to Visit: Open daily from 8 AM to 6 PM; perfect for a shopping break after snorkeling or beach time
What to Expect: This gift shop, located at the Anse Chastanet Resort, offers a great selection of quality souvenirs and locally made products. It's a bit pricier than the local markets, but you'll find high-quality items and unique pieces that make it worth a visit.

Top Souvenirs to Buy:

- <u>Handcrafted Jewelry</u>: Look for pieces made with local seashells and beads.
- <u>St. Lucian Cocoa Products</u>: The shop sells locally made chocolate bars and cocoa tea mixes—great for food lovers.
- <u>Beachwear</u>: Pick up a stylish sarong or beach hat as a practical souvenir.

<u>Pro Tip:</u> Combine your visit with a snorkeling session at Anse Chastanet Beach—one of the best spots on the island for exploring coral reefs.

C. Tips for Bargaining and Finding Authentic Goods

1. Know Where to Bargain (and Where Not To)

In St. Lucia, bargaining is generally accepted and even expected in local markets like Castries Market and the Choiseul Craft Market. Vendors often set initial prices higher, anticipating that customers will negotiate. However, bargaining is less common in fixed-price stores, duty-free shops, and higher-end boutiques, so it's best to respect the pricing in these places.

<u>Pro Tip:</u> When bargaining, start by offering about 20-30% below the asking price. This gives you room to negotiate while remaining respectful. Keep the tone friendly and light—it's all part of the experience!

2. Look for Local Craftsmanship

St. Lucia has a thriving artisan community, and you'll find many unique, handcrafted items made by local artists. However, some vendors may sell imported goods that aren't genuinely representative of the island's culture. To ensure you're buying authentic St. Lucian products, look for items made from local materials like mahogany wood, calabash, coconut shells, and woven pandanus leaves.

- <u>What to Buy:</u> Hand-carved wooden sculptures, pottery, handwoven baskets, and locally made jewelry are all great options. These items are often created using traditional techniques passed down through generations, making them true pieces of St. Lucian heritage.

<u>Pro Tip</u>: Ask the vendor about the origin of the item and the artist who made it. Authentic pieces often come with a story, and vendors are usually proud to share the history behind their crafts.

3. Timing Is Everything

The best time to shop at local markets is in the early morning, when vendors are setting up for the day. You'll have the first pick of fresh goods and souvenirs, and vendors may be more open to negotiating as they look to make their first sales (often considered good luck). Shopping later in the day can still be fruitful, especially if vendors are looking to clear out stock before closing.

Pro Tip: If you're shopping during the peak tourist season (December to April), aim to visit on weekdays when markets are less crowded. This will give you a better chance to browse leisurely and engage in friendly negotiations.

4. Be Respectful and Build Rapport

Bargaining in St. Lucia is a social activity as much as it is a transaction. Take a moment to greet the vendor and ask about their day before jumping into price discussions. Showing genuine interest and friendliness goes a long way and can often lead to better deals.

Pro Tip: Learn a few basic phrases in Kwéyòl (Creole), such as "Bonjou" (Good morning) and "Mesi" (Thank you). Vendors appreciate the effort and may be more willing to offer you a fair price.

5. Pay in Local Currency When Possible

While many vendors accept US dollars, you'll often get a better deal if you pay in Eastern Caribbean dollars (EC$), the local currency. Using local currency can help you avoid unfavorable exchange rates and show that you're familiar with local customs, which may make vendors more open to negotiating.

Pro Tip: Carry small bills and change in EC dollars. It's easier for vendors to handle, and having exact change can sometimes help you secure a slightly better price.

6. Know the Authentic Items and Avoid Mass-Produced Souvenirs

To ensure you're buying genuine St. Lucian crafts, look for signs of handmade quality, such as slight imperfections or variations in color and texture. Avoid items that look overly uniform, as these are often mass-produced imports rather than locally made pieces. Some common authentic items include:

- Cocoa Sticks: Handmade from locally grown cocoa, these sticks are used to make traditional St. Lucian cocoa tea—a unique and delicious souvenir.
- Hot Pepper Sauce: Look for small, locally branded bottles featuring vibrant colors and fresh ingredients. These sauces make great gifts for spice lovers.
- Chairman's Reserve Rum or Bounty Rum: These local rums are top-quality souvenirs that offer a true taste of the island. Always buy from reputable stores or duty-free shops to ensure authenticity.

7. Don't Be Afraid to Walk Away

If you can't agree on a price, don't hesitate to politely thank the vendor and walk away. Often, vendors will call you back with a better offer if they're willing to negotiate further. If not, you'll know you've reached their lowest price. It's all part of the friendly bargaining process, so keep it light and fun.

Pro Tip: If you see something you love, but the price seems steep, take a lap around the market first. You might find similar items at different stalls, giving you a better idea of the going rate before you commit.

8. Keep an Eye Out for Special Deals

Many markets and shops in St. Lucia offer bundle deals or discounts if you buy multiple items. If you're planning to purchase several souvenirs, ask the vendor if they can offer a deal for buying in bulk.

- Pro Tip: Politely ask, "Can you give me a better price if I buy two?" or "Do you have any special offers today?" You'd be surprised how often vendors are willing to offer a little extra discount, especially if you're buying gifts for friends and family

216

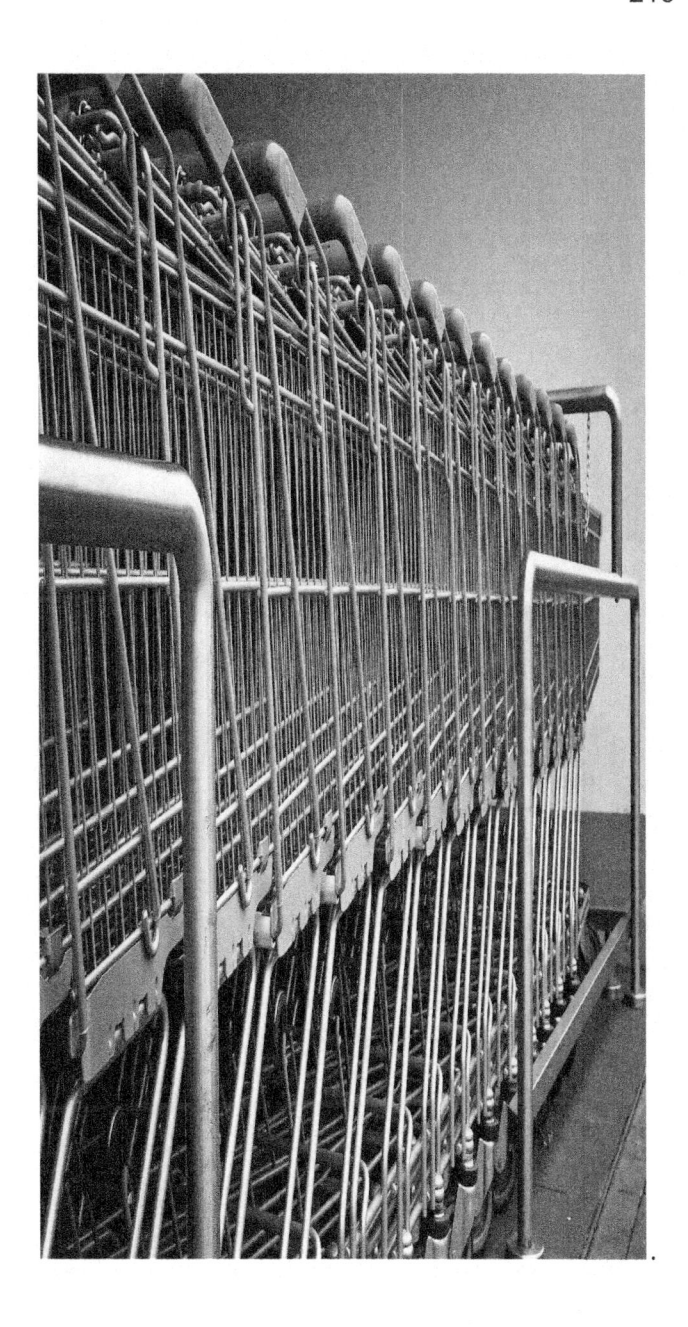

Chapter 12: Family Travel in St. Lucia

A. Kid-Friendly Attractions and Activities

Hey there, family adventurer! If you're planning a trip to St. Lucia with kids, you're in for a fun-filled vacation that everyone will enjoy. Let's dive into the best kid-friendly attractions and activities to make your family getaway unforgettable!

1. Splash Island Water Park

- Location: Reduit Beach, Rodney Bay
- Best Time to Visit: Open daily from 9 AM to 5 PM; visit early in the morning or late in the afternoon to avoid the heat
- What to Expect: Splash Island Water Park is a floating obstacle course that's sure to be a hit with the kids. It's an inflatable water park set right in the ocean,

featuring slides, trampolines, climbing walls, and monkey bars. It's designed for kids aged 6 and up, but adults can join in the fun too. It's a great way to spend a few hours letting the kids burn off some energy while you relax on the nearby beach.

- Price: $15 - $20 USD per hour per person

Pro Tip: Bring sunscreen and water shoes—the inflatable structures can get slippery, and the sun can be intense. There are lifeguards on duty, but it's still a good idea to keep a close eye on younger kids.

2. Pigeon Island National Park

- Location: Near Gros Islet, accessible via a short causeway from the mainland
- Best Time to Visit: Open daily from 9 AM to 5 PM; visit in the morning for cooler weather and fewer crowds
- What to Expect: Pigeon Island National Park is a fantastic spot for families who love a mix of history and outdoor activities. The park features old military ruins that kids can explore, including the historic Fort Rodney. The short hike to the fort is manageable for kids and offers incredible views of the surrounding coastline. There are also two beautiful beaches perfect for swimming, snorkeling, and building sandcastles.

- Price: $10 USD per adult, $3 USD per child (kids under 5 are free)

Pro Tip: Pack a picnic lunch to enjoy in the shaded picnic areas, or stop by the on-site restaurant for a kid-friendly meal. Bring snorkeling gear for the kids to explore the clear, shallow waters near the beach.

3. Diamond Falls Botanical Gardens

- Location: Soufrière, near the Diamond Falls and Sulphur Springs
- Best Time to Visit: Open daily from 10 AM to 5 PM; visit early to avoid the midday heat
- What to Expect: For a more relaxed family outing, head to the Diamond Falls Botanical Gardens. It's a beautiful, shaded garden featuring vibrant tropical plants and flowers that kids will love exploring. The highlight of the visit is the Diamond Waterfall, a colorful, mineral-rich waterfall that changes color due to the volcanic minerals in the water. Kids will enjoy spotting butterflies, hummingbirds, and other wildlife along the paths.

- Price: $7 USD per adult, $3 USD per child

Pro Tip: Combine your visit with a stop at the nearby Sulphur Springs, where older kids can experience the unique "drive-in volcano" and take a dip in the warm, mineral-rich mud baths.

4. Treetop Adventure Park

- <u>Location</u>: Dennery Valley, on the east coast of the island
- <u>Best Time to Visit:</u> Open daily from 9 AM to 4 PM; book your tour in advance, especially during peak season
- <u>What to Expect:</u> If your kids love adventure, they'll have a blast at Treetop Adventure Park. The park features a series of zip lines that take you soaring through the rainforest canopy. It's a thrilling experience that's safe for kids aged 5 and up. The park provides all the safety gear and offers a quick training session before you start. It's a great way to enjoy the island's natural beauty while getting a bit of exercise.

- <u>Price:</u> $75 USD per adult, $50 USD per child

<u>Pro Tip:</u> Wear closed-toe shoes and comfortable clothing. The guides are fantastic with kids and make sure everyone feels safe and confident before starting the zip lines.

5. Rodney Bay Marina

- <u>Location</u>: Rodney Bay, Gros Islet
- <u>Best Time to Visit:</u> Open daily, with boat tours departing throughout the day

- <u>What to Expect:</u> For a fun family outing on the water, head to Rodney Bay Marina, where you can book a variety of boat tours perfect for kids. One of the highlights is the Pirate Adventure Cruise, a themed boat tour where kids can dress up as pirates, learn to tie knots, and even have a mock pirate battle. It's a fantastic way for kids to learn about the island's maritime history while having a blast.

- <u>Price:</u> Pirate cruises typically cost $50 - $70 USD per person, depending on the tour length

<u>Pro Tip:</u> Bring swimsuits and towels, as many tours include stops for swimming and snorkeling. Don't forget sunscreen and hats for sun protection on the open water.

Tips for Enjoying Family Activities in St. Lucia

- <u>Pack Snacks and Water:</u> While many attractions have cafés, it's always a good idea to bring snacks and water, especially if you have younger kids who might get hungry between meals.
- <u>Dress Comfortably:</u> Lightweight, breathable clothing and good walking shoes are essential for exploring. Don't forget hats and sunglasses for sun protection.
- <u>Plan Ahead:</u> Some activities, like the Pirate Adventure Cruise and zip-lining, require

reservations. Book in advance to secure your spot and avoid disappointment.

B. Family-Friendly Accommodations

1. Coconut Bay Beach Resort & Spa

- Location: Vieux Fort, on the southeastern coast, just a 5-minute drive from Hewanorra International Airport
- What to Expect: Coconut Bay Beach Resort & Spa is one of the best all-inclusive resorts for families in St. Lucia. The resort is divided into two sections: Harmony for adults and Splash for families. The Splash side features a massive water park with slides, a lazy river, and a splash pad—perfect for keeping the kids entertained. There's also a Kid's Club with supervised activities, crafts, and games, giving parents some time to relax.

- Room Types: Choose from spacious family rooms with bunk beds or interconnecting suites for extra space.
- Dining: Enjoy a variety of dining options, including kid-friendly buffets and a pizza restaurant. All meals, snacks, and drinks are included in the all-inclusive package.

- **Price Range:** Rates start at $400 - $700 USD per night for a family suite, depending on the season.
- **Pro Tip:** Book a room on the Splash side for easy access to the water park and kid's activities. Take advantage of the included kite-surfing lessons and beachfront games for added fun.

2. The Landings Resort & Spa

- **Location:** Rodney Bay, on the northern coast of the island
- **What to Expect:** The Landings Resort & Spa is a luxury beachfront property that's perfect for families seeking a home-away-from-home experience. The resort features spacious two- and three-bedroom villas, complete with full kitchens, living areas, and private balconies. Kids will love the Kid's Club, which offers arts and crafts, beach games, and nature walks. The resort also has a beautiful beach, multiple pools, and a range of water sports available.

- **Room Types:** Two- and three-bedroom villas with options for beachfront or marina views.
- **Dining:** On-site restaurants offer a variety of cuisines, with plenty of kid-friendly options like pasta, burgers, and fresh fruit smoothies.

- **Price Range:** Villas start at $500 - $1,200 USD per night, depending on the size and view.

Pro Tip: Take advantage of the grocery delivery service if you want to cook some meals in your villa's kitchen. It's a great way to save money and enjoy a cozy family meal.

3. Bay Gardens Beach Resort

- **Location:** Reduit Beach, Rodney Bay
- **What to Expect:** For families seeking a more affordable yet fun-packed option, Bay Gardens Beach Resort is an excellent choice. Located right on the beautiful Reduit Beach, this resort offers easy access to the Splash Island Water Park, which kids will love. The resort has a kid's pool, daily activities, and even a free shuttle to its sister properties for more dining and entertainment options.
- **Room Types:** Choose from family suites with kitchenettes or interconnecting rooms for larger groups.
- **Dining:** Several on-site restaurants offer a mix of Caribbean and international dishes. Kids' menus are available, and the beachfront dining is a big hit with families.
- **Price Range:** Rates start at $250 - $450 USD per night, making it a great value for families.

Pro Tip: Book the All-Inclusive Family Package, which includes unlimited access to the Splash Island Water Park, non-motorized water sports, and complimentary babysitting for up to 2 hours per day.

4. Windjammer Landing Villa Beach Resort

- Location: Labrelotte Bay, just north of Castries
- What to Expect: Windjammer Landing is a stunning beachfront resort offering a variety of accommodations, including spacious villas that are perfect for families. The resort has a great kid's program called Windjammer Kids Club, featuring activities like treasure hunts, sandcastle building, and cooking classes. Teens can enjoy water sports like kayaking, snorkeling, and paddleboarding. The multiple pools, including a kid-friendly pool, offer plenty of space for family fun.

- Room Types: Family villas with up to four bedrooms, private terraces, and some with private plunge pools.
- Dining: Six on-site restaurants offer a wide range of choices, from Italian to Caribbean cuisine. Kids' meals and special dietary options are available.

- Price Range: Villas start at $400 - $1,000 USD per night, depending on size and season.

Pro Tip: Book a villa with a private plunge pool for added privacy and fun for the kids. Don't miss the resort's family movie night on the beach—it's a hit with both kids and parents.

5. Sugar Beach, A Viceroy Resort

- Location: Between the iconic Pitons, near Soufrière
- What to Expect: If you're looking to splurge on a luxury family vacation, Sugar Beach, A Viceroy Resort is the place to go. Nestled between the Pitons, this resort offers breathtaking views, luxury accommodations, and top-notch amenities. The Sugar Club for kids features activities like arts and crafts, storytelling, and nature walks, while older kids and teens can enjoy kayaking, paddleboarding, and guided hikes.
- Room Types: Luxury cottages and villas with private pools and butler service.
- Dining: Several high-end dining options, including kid-friendly menus and gourmet picnic setups for a memorable beach meal.
- Price Range: Rates start at $800 - $2,500 USD per night, depending on the season and accommodation type.

Pro Tip: Take advantage of the babysitting service for a date night at the fine dining restaurant. It's a great way to enjoy a romantic evening while the kids have fun at the club.

C. Safety Tips for Traveling with Children

1. Sun Safety: Protect Your Little Ones from the Caribbean Sun

The Caribbean sun is strong, and it's easy for kids to get sunburned, especially when they're busy playing in the water or building sandcastles. To avoid sunburn and heat-related issues, make sure you're prepared with plenty of sunscreen, hats, and protective clothing.

- Sunscreen: Use a broad-spectrum sunscreen with at least SPF 30. Reapply every two hours, especially after swimming or sweating.
- Hats and Sunglasses: Pack wide-brimmed hats and UV-protective sunglasses for extra protection.
- Stay Hydrated: Make sure everyone drinks plenty of water throughout the day, as dehydration can sneak up quickly in hot weather. Bring refillable water bottles and keep them handy.

Pro Tip: Plan outdoor activities for the early morning or late afternoon to avoid the peak sun hours (10 AM to 2 PM). If you're at the beach, look for shaded areas or bring an umbrella.

2. Water Safety: Stay Safe at the Beach and Pool

St. Lucia's beaches and pools are a big draw for families, but it's important to keep water safety in mind, especially with young children. While many resorts have lifeguards, it's best not to rely solely on them and to keep a close eye on your kids at all times.

- Supervision: Always supervise children when they're in or near the water, even if they're good swimmers. The ocean can have strong currents, especially at beaches with open water.
- Swim Gear: Consider bringing floaties or a life jacket for younger kids who aren't strong swimmers yet. Many hotels and resorts offer pool noodles and other swim aids, but it's always good to have your own.
- Know the Beach Conditions: Check with locals or hotel staff about the current beach conditions. Some beaches may have strong undertows or be more suitable for experienced swimmers.

Pro Tip: Red and yellow flags indicate safe swimming areas, while red flags mean the water is dangerous. Stick to designated swimming zones and follow the lifeguard's instructions.

3. Health and Safety: Prepare for Minor Illnesses and Emergencies

When traveling with children, it's always a good idea to be prepared for minor illnesses or unexpected medical needs. St. Lucia has good healthcare facilities, but it's best to pack a basic first-aid kit for any minor injuries or illnesses that may occur during your trip.

- First-Aid Kit Essentials: Pack band-aids, antiseptic wipes, pain relievers (like acetaminophen or ibuprofen), motion sickness medication, and any necessary prescription medications. If your child has allergies, don't forget their EpiPen or allergy medication.
- Travel Insurance: Make sure your travel insurance covers medical emergencies, and keep a copy of your policy and emergency contact numbers with you.
- Local Pharmacies: Pharmacies are available in most towns and tourist areas, including Castries and Rodney Bay. They carry common medications and first-aid supplies.

Pro Tip: Download a map of nearby medical facilities or ask your hotel for recommendations on the closest hospital or clinic in case of an emergency.

4. Food and Drink Safety: Keep Kids Healthy on the Go

St. Lucia offers a variety of delicious foods and beverages that your kids will love. However, it's important to be cautious with certain foods and drinks to avoid any stomach issues during your vacation.

- <u>Safe Drinking Water</u>: Stick to bottled or filtered water for drinking, especially for young children. Most resorts provide bottled water, and it's widely available in stores.
- <u>Be Cautious with Street Food:</u> While St. Lucia's street food is tasty and tempting, choose vendors with good hygiene practices. Opt for cooked foods and avoid raw or undercooked items like seafood.
- <u>Introduce New Foods Slowly:</u> If your child has a sensitive stomach, introduce new foods gradually to avoid any digestive issues. Keep snacks like crackers, applesauce, or granola bars handy for picky eaters.

<u>Pro Tip:</u> Always wash your hands or use hand sanitizer before meals, especially when dining outdoors or at street vendors.

5. Transportation Safety: Getting Around Safely with Kids

Whether you're taking a taxi, renting a car, or using local buses, transportation safety is key when traveling with kids in St. Lucia. Roads can be narrow and winding, so it's important to plan ahead and choose reliable transportation options.

- Car Seats: If you're renting a car, request a car seat or bring your own. Not all taxis have car seats, so it's best to arrange a transfer with a service that can provide one if needed.
- Seat Belts: Make sure everyone buckles up, even for short trips. Taxis and private shuttles are common, but always check that the vehicle has functioning seat belts.
- Choose Reputable Transport: Use hotel-recommended taxi services or book through a reputable tour company for day trips. The public buses can be a fun experience, but they may not have seat belts or air conditioning.

Pro Tip: If you're planning a lot of driving, consider renting a larger vehicle for more comfort and safety, especially on the island's steep and winding roads.

232

Chapter 13: Travel Tips and Resources

A. Travel Apps and Online Resources

1. Google Maps

- <u>Why You Need It</u>: While St. Lucia is a relatively small island, its winding roads and hidden beaches can be tricky to navigate. Google Maps is an invaluable tool for helping you find your way around, whether you're driving a rental car, taking a taxi, or exploring on foot. It's also great for finding the best-rated restaurants, attractions, and gas stations along your route.

- <u>How to Use It</u>: Download offline maps of St. Lucia before your trip so you can navigate even without a data connection. This is especially useful when exploring remote areas or hiking near the Pitons.

<u>Pro Tip</u>: Use the "Explore" feature to discover nearby attractions, eateries, and local events based on your location. It's a handy way to stumble upon hidden gems you might otherwise miss.

2. TripAdvisor

- <u>Why You Need It</u>: TripAdvisor is a go-to resource for finding honest reviews and recommendations for hotels, restaurants, and tours in St. Lucia. It's great for getting a feel for what to expect before you book an excursion or make a dinner reservation.

- <u>How to Use It</u>: Search for the top-rated activities, read recent traveler reviews, and check out photos uploaded by other visitors. Use the "Near Me Now" feature to find the best places around your current location.

<u>Pro Tip</u>: Don't just look at the star rating—read through the latest reviews to get detailed insights and tips from fellow travelers. Look for reviews from families if you're traveling with kids, as they often mention kid-friendly amenities.

3. WhatsApp

- <u>Why You Need It</u>: WhatsApp is a must-have app for staying connected with both local contacts and friends or family back home. It's widely used in St. Lucia for messaging and making free calls over Wi-Fi, making it a great way to avoid hefty international roaming charges.

- <u>How to Use It</u>: Download WhatsApp before your trip and add your contacts.

Use it for messaging, voice calls, and video calls, especially if you're relying on hotel Wi-Fi or a local SIM card.

Pro Tip: Save the numbers of your hotel, tour guides, and taxi drivers on WhatsApp. Many local businesses use the app for easy communication and quick responses.

4. XE Currency Converter

- Why You Need It: XE Currency Converter is a handy app for quickly converting Eastern Caribbean dollars (EC$) to your home currency. This is especially useful when shopping at local markets, paying for street food, or budgeting for excursions.

- How to Use It: Enter the amount you want to convert, and the app will show you the equivalent in your chosen currency based on the latest exchange rate. You can also save favorite conversions for quick access.

Pro Tip: Download the offline rates feature so you can access exchange rates even without an internet connection. This is great for shopping in areas with limited cell service.

5. Google Translate

- Why You Need It: While English is widely spoken in St. Lucia, you might encounter locals speaking Kwéyòl (Creole), especially in more rural areas or during cultural events. Google Translate can help you understand simple phrases and communicate with locals.

- <u>How to Use It:</u> Use the voice or text input feature for quick translations. Download the offline Creole translation pack before your trip so you can use it even when you don't have internet access.

<u>Pro Tip:</u> Try the camera translation feature—it lets you point your phone's camera at text (like menus or signs) and instantly see the translation on your screen. It's a lifesaver when navigating local markets or reading menus at Creole restaurants.

6. Viator and GetYourGuide

- <u>Why You Need It:</u> If you're looking to book guided tours, excursions, or adventure activities, Viator and GetYourGuide are two of the best platforms to use. They offer a wide range of options, from zip-lining adventures to catamaran cruises, all with detailed reviews and booking options.

- <u>How to Use It:</u> Browse through the available tours, read reviews, and book directly through the app. Most bookings come with free cancellation options, which is great for flexible travel plans.

Pro Tip: Look for package deals or discounts, especially if you're planning multiple activities. Booking through the app often comes with extra perks like hotel pick-up or skip-the-line access.

7. Waze

- Why You Need It: If you're renting a car in St. Lucia, Waze is a great app for navigating the island's roads. It offers real-time traffic updates, road conditions, and alerts for speed cameras or hazards, making it a helpful tool for safe driving.

- How to Use It: Enter your destination, and Waze will give you the fastest route based on current traffic conditions. It's especially useful during peak travel times or if there's road construction.

Pro Tip: Turn on voice navigation so you can keep your eyes on the road. It's safer and helps you focus on driving, especially on the island's narrow, winding roads.

8. MySOS

- Why You Need It: MySOS is a valuable app for accessing emergency contacts and medical information in unfamiliar destinations. It provides a list of nearby hospitals, clinics, and emergency services, which can be reassuring when traveling with kids or elderly family members.

- How to Use It: Set up your emergency contacts and medical information before your trip. The app uses your location to show the nearest medical facilities and emergency numbers.

Pro Tip: Save the local emergency number for St. Lucia (911) in your phone, and make sure everyone in your family knows where to find it.

B. Packing Tips for St. Lucia

1. Lightweight, Breathable Clothing

St. Lucia's tropical climate means warm temperatures year-round, so pack lightweight and breathable clothing to keep comfortable. Think cotton t-shirts, tank tops, shorts, and light dresses. Fabrics like linen and moisture-wicking materials are perfect for staying cool and dry, especially if you plan to do any hiking or outdoor activities.

- Pro Tip: Pack a couple of dressier outfits for dining at upscale restaurants or attending special events. Many resorts and restaurants have a "smart casual" dress code for dinner, so a nice sundress, collared shirt, or polo will do the trick.

2. Swimwear and Beach Essentials

You'll be spending a lot of time at the beach or pool, so bring at least two swimsuits to rotate between. It's also a good idea to pack a cover-up, sun hat, and UV-protective sunglasses for extra sun protection. A quick-dry towel and waterproof beach bag are handy for beach days or boat trips.

- Pro Tip: Don't forget to pack reef-safe sunscreen (SPF 30 or higher). Regular sunscreens can damage coral reefs, so choose a product that's safe for the environment. Sunscreen is expensive on the island, so it's better to bring enough from home.

3. Footwear

Choose your footwear based on the activities you plan to do. For beach days, bring flip-flops or water sandals that are easy to slip on and off. If you plan to hike or explore the rainforests, pack a pair of sturdy walking shoes or hiking sandals with good grip. For evenings out, bring a pair of casual yet stylish sandals or loafers.

- Pro Tip: Break in your hiking shoes before the trip to avoid blisters. Pack anti-chafe sticks or band-aids if you're planning long walks or hikes.

4. Adventure Gear

If you're planning on snorkeling, kayaking, or exploring underwater caves, consider bringing your own snorkel mask and fins. While rental gear is available, having your own set ensures a proper fit and better hygiene. For hiking, pack a light daypack to carry water, snacks, and your essentials. Don't forget a waterproof phone case or dry bag for keeping electronics safe during water activities.

- <u>Pro Tip:</u> Bring a refillable water bottle with a built-in filter. Staying hydrated is key, and filtered bottles help ensure you're drinking safe, clean water.

5. Sun and Insect Protection

In addition to sunscreen, pack an after-sun lotion like aloe vera gel for soothing sun-exposed skin. Mosquitoes can be an issue, especially in the evenings and near the rainforests, so bring a good insect repellent with DEET or natural options like lemon eucalyptus oil.

- <u>Pro Tip:</u> Consider packing anti-itch cream or antihistamine tablets in case of bug bites. A small first-aid kit with essentials like band-aids, antiseptic wipes, and pain relievers is also a good idea.

6. Electronics and Travel Gadgets

Bring a good-quality camera or smartphone to capture the stunning scenery. Pack an extra memory card and a portable power bank to keep your devices charged throughout the day. If you plan to do any water activities, consider a GoPro or waterproof camera for underwater shots.

- <u>Pro Tip</u>: Bring a universal travel adapter, as the electrical outlets in St. Lucia may differ from those in your home country. Most hotels use 220V British-style plugs (Type G), so double-check before you go.

7. Documents and Essentials

Keep all your important documents organized in a travel wallet or folder. This includes your passport, travel insurance, flight details, and any reservation confirmations. Don't forget a copy of your COVID-19 vaccination card or test results if required. It's also a good idea to bring a small amount of local currency (Eastern Caribbean dollars) for small purchases and tips.

- <u>Pro Tip:</u> Make digital copies of your important documents and save them on your phone or email them to yourself. This way, you'll have a backup if anything gets lost.

8. Packing Tips for the Rainy Season

St. Lucia's rainy season runs from June to November, but don't worry—it usually just means short, refreshing showers. Pack a light rain jacket or poncho and a compact travel umbrella. Quick-dry clothing is also a plus, as it helps you stay comfortable even if you get caught in the rain.

- <u>Pro Tip</u>: Use packing cubes or compression bags to organize your suitcase and save space. Keep a separate plastic bag for wet clothes or swimsuits after a day at the beach.

C. Staying Connected

1. Local SIM Cards

One of the best ways to stay connected in St. Lucia is by purchasing a local SIM card. It's a cost-effective option that provides access to local data plans, making it easy to use GPS, send messages, and browse the web without relying on expensive international roaming.

- <u>Where to Buy:</u> You can purchase SIM cards at the Hewanorra International Airport (UVF) upon arrival, or at mobile provider stores in Castries and Rodney Bay. The two main providers are Digicel and FLOW.

- Cost: A basic SIM card typically costs around $10 USD, with data plans starting at $10 - $25 USD for a week of unlimited data or a set amount of GBs.
- What You Need: You'll need your passport to register the SIM card. Most SIM cards are prepaid and can be topped up at convenience stores, gas stations, or online.

Pro Tip: Make sure your phone is unlocked before your trip so it can accept a foreign SIM card. If you're staying for a week or longer, look for special tourist plans that offer good value for short-term visitors.

2. Wi-Fi Access

Wi-Fi is widely available in St. Lucia, especially in tourist areas. Most hotels, resorts, and guesthouses offer free Wi-Fi in rooms and common areas. While the connection can be strong in larger towns like Castries, Soufrière, and Rodney Bay, expect slower speeds or limited access in more remote parts of the island.

- Best Places for Wi-Fi: In addition to your hotel, many cafés, restaurants, and bars offer free Wi-Fi for customers. Popular spots like Bay Gardens Beach Resort and The Naked Fisherman provide reliable connections.

- Pro Tip: If you need a strong connection for work or video calls, head to a café like Café Ole in Rodney Bay, which is known for its good Wi-Fi and cozy atmosphere.

3. Mobile Hotspots and Data Plans

If you need reliable internet access throughout the island, consider renting a mobile hotspot device. This portable Wi-Fi device connects to the local mobile network and creates a secure hotspot that you can use with multiple devices. It's a great option for families or groups who need to stay connected without using multiple SIM cards.

- Where to Rent: You can rent mobile hotspots at the airport or from local providers like Digicel and FLOW. Some rental car companies and hotels also offer them as an add-on service.
- Cost: Rental fees start at around $10 - $15 USD per day, with unlimited data plans available for an extra charge.

Pro Tip: Check if your hotel offers a mobile hotspot rental service as part of their amenities. It might be included for free, especially at higher-end resorts.

4. International Roaming

If you prefer not to switch SIM cards, you can use your current phone plan with international roaming. However, roaming charges can add up quickly, so it's essential to check with your carrier before your trip to see what options are available.

- <u>How to Use It</u>: Most major U.S. carriers like Verizon, AT&T, and T-Mobile offer international roaming plans that include St. Lucia. Plans may include a daily fee (usually $10 - $15 USD per day) for unlimited calls, texts, and data.

<u>Pro Tip:</u> If you only need to use your phone occasionally, disable data roaming in your settings and connect to Wi-Fi whenever possible to avoid unexpected charges.

5. Using Offline Maps and Apps

If you're worried about staying connected while exploring more remote areas of St. Lucia, consider downloading offline maps and apps before you leave. Apps like Google Maps, Maps.me, and TripAdvisor allow you to save maps and information for offline use, making it easy to navigate even without an internet connection.

<u>Pro Tip</u>: Download offline maps of St. Lucia and save your hotel details, key attractions, and restaurant recommendations before your trip. It's a great backup plan if you find yourself without internet access.

6. Emergency Access

In case of an emergency, it's good to know how to quickly access internet services or contact local authorities. Many hotels and resorts offer complimentary phone services for emergency calls, and most towns have internet cafés where you can get online in a pinch.

- <u>Local Emergency Number:</u> 911 is the emergency contact number in St. Lucia for police, fire, and medical assistance.

<u>Pro Tip:</u> Keep a list of your important contacts saved offline, including your hotel's phone number, tour operators, and emergency services.

D. Emergency Contacts and Useful Numbers

1. Emergency Services: Police, Fire, and Medical Assistance

St. Lucia has a unified emergency contact number for police, fire, and medical services. If you find yourself in an urgent situation, dial 911 from any phone. This number is accessible throughout the island and is the quickest way to reach emergency personnel.

- <u>Emergency Number</u>: 911 (Police, Fire, Ambulance)
- <u>When to Use It:</u> Call 911 for any life-threatening emergency, including

accidents, serious illnesses, or if you feel your personal safety is at risk.

Pro Tip: Keep a list of emergency numbers saved on your phone and written down in your travel documents. It's helpful in case your phone battery dies or you don't have access to your usual contacts.

2. Nearest Hospitals and Medical Facilities

St. Lucia has several well-equipped hospitals and medical centers that provide quality care to both locals and tourists. The main hospitals are located in Castries and Vieux Fort, with smaller clinics available in other towns.

Tapion Hospital (Castries): A private hospital known for its excellent services. Ideal for non-emergency medical needs like minor injuries or illnesses.
- Contact: +1 (758) 459-2000
- Address: Tapion Hill, Castries
- Pro Tip: Private hospitals may require upfront payment or proof of travel insurance, so keep your insurance details handy.

Victoria Hospital (Castries): The main public hospital offering a range of medical services, including emergency care.
- Contact: +1 (758) 452-2421
- Address: Millennium Highway, Castries

- <u>Pro Tip</u>: This hospital is best for emergency care, but expect longer wait times than at private facilities.

<u>St. Jude Hospital (Vieux Fort)</u>: Serving the southern part of the island, this hospital handles both emergency and routine medical cases.
- <u>Contact</u>: +1 (758) 454-6041
- <u>Address</u>: Augier, Vieux Fort
- <u>Pro Tip</u>: If you're staying in the south, St. Jude Hospital is the quickest option for medical emergencies.

3. Contacting the Police

While St. Lucia is generally a safe destination, it's always good to know how to reach the police if needed. The Royal St. Lucia Police Force is professional and responsive, handling everything from lost items to serious incidents.

<u>Non-Emergency Police Contact:</u> +1 (758) 456-3990 (Castries Police Station)
- <u>Tourist Police:</u> There are dedicated officers who assist tourists with issues like lost passports, minor theft, or safety concerns. You can find them in popular areas like Rodney Bay and Soufrière.

<u>Pro Tip</u>: If you lose your passport, contact the nearest police station to file a report. You'll need a police report for your embassy to issue a replacement.

4. Embassies and Consulates

If you lose your passport, need travel assistance, or face legal issues, your country's embassy or consulate can provide support. St. Lucia hosts several consular offices, and many other countries have embassies based in nearby Barbados or Trinidad and Tobago.

U.S. Embassy (Bridgetown, Barbados): Covers St. Lucia; provides services like passport replacement and emergency assistance.
- Contact: +1 (246) 227-4000
- Website: bb.usembassy.gov

British High Commission (Castries): Offers support for British citizens, including legal assistance and travel advice.
- Contact: +1 (758) 452-2484
- Address: Barnard Hill, Castries

Canadian Consulate (Castries): Provides consular services for Canadians visiting St. Lucia.
- Contact: +1 (758) 452-3271
- Address: Barnard Hill, Castries

Pro Tip: Save your embassy's phone number and email address before you travel. In an emergency, they can assist with lost documents, legal issues, and providing advice.

5. Tourist Assistance

For general travel inquiries or issues that aren't emergencies, the St. Lucia Tourist Board is a great resource. They can provide information about local events, attractions, and travel advice.

St. Lucia Tourist Board Contact: +1 (758) 452-4094
- Website: stlucia.org

Pro Tip: If you're unsure where to go for assistance, start with a call to the Tourist Board. They can often direct you to the right contact or service.

6. Travel Insurance

Travel insurance is a must when visiting St. Lucia, especially if you plan on doing activities like hiking, zip-lining, or snorkeling. Your policy should cover medical emergencies, trip cancellations, and lost belongings. Keep a copy of your insurance policy and contact numbers with you at all times.

- Pro Tip: If you need to use your travel insurance, call your provider's emergency assistance line first. They can help coordinate care and direct you to the nearest approved medical facility.

Conclusion

Congratulations on Choosing the **St. Lucia Travel Guide 2025**! We're thrilled that you've chosen this guide to help you explore one of the Caribbean's most captivating islands. St. Lucia is a paradise of lush landscapes, vibrant culture, and unforgettable experiences, and we hope this book has made your journey easier, more enriching, and filled with beautiful memories.

Throughout these pages, we've taken you on a tour of St. Lucia's must-see spots—from the iconic Pitons that dominate the skyline to the bustling energy of Castries, and from the tranquil beaches of Marigot Bay to the charming fishing villages like Soufrière and Anse La Raye. Each corner of the island has its own story, and we hope our insights have helped you uncover the unique character of each place.

This guide introduced you to St. Lucia's incredible natural beauty and wildlife, guiding you to the best spots for snorkeling among colorful reefs, hiking through lush rainforests, and relaxing on pristine sandy shores. The island's vibrant flora and fauna offer a sense of adventure and discovery that we hope you've experienced firsthand.

But St. Lucia is more than just its stunning landscapes. It's a place rich in history and culture, from the legacy of its indigenous Arawak and Carib peoples to the influences of French and British settlers. We hope that learning about St. Lucia's past has deepened your connection to the island and its people.

We've also included practical tips and recommendations to make your travels seamless, from finding the perfect accommodations to navigating transportation options around the island. Whether you chose to stay in a luxury resort, a boutique guesthouse, or a cozy beachside villa, we hope our suggestions helped you enjoy St. Lucia to the fullest.

As you wrap up your visit, we hope you leave with cherished memories of St. Lucia's sparkling waters, vibrant markets, and the warmth of its people. This island isn't just a place to see—it's a feeling you take with you, one of joy, relaxation, and a deep sense of discovery.

Thank you for letting the St. Lucia Travel Guide 2025 be a part of your adventure. May the spirit of St. Lucia stay with you, and may your travels continue to be filled with incredible experiences and discoveries.

Safe travels, and we hope to welcome you back to St. Lucia soon!

Warm regards,

The St. Lucia Travel Guide 2025 Team

Bonus: Authentic St. Lucian Recipes

As a special bonus, we're excited to share some of St. Lucia's beloved traditional recipes. Each dish reflects the vibrant culture and rich culinary heritage of the island, featuring fresh seafood, local spices, and tropical ingredients. These recipes offer a true taste of St. Lucia—flavorful, comforting, and deeply connected to its people and traditions.

1. Green Fig and Saltfish

This is St. Lucia's national dish, made with salted cod and boiled green bananas (known locally as "green figs"). It's a hearty, savory meal that's enjoyed throughout the island, often for breakfast or lunch.

Ingredients:
- 1 lb salted codfish
- 6 green bananas, peeled
- 1 onion, diced
- 1 bell pepper, diced
- 2 cloves garlic, minced
- 2 tomatoes, chopped
- 2 tbsp olive oil
- Fresh thyme
- Black pepper to taste

Instructions:

1. Soak the salted codfish in water overnight to remove excess salt. Drain and rinse well.
2. Boil the codfish for 10 minutes, drain, and flake into small pieces.
3. In a separate pot, boil the green bananas until tender, then drain and slice.
4. Heat olive oil in a pan, sauté the onions, garlic, bell pepper, and tomatoes until soft.
5. Add the flaked codfish, thyme, and black pepper. Stir well and cook for another 5 minutes.
6. Serve the saltfish mixture over the sliced green bananas.

2. Accra (Saltfish Fritters)

These crispy, flavorful fritters are a favorite street food in St. Lucia, made with salted cod and seasoned with herbs and spices. They're perfect as a snack or appetizer.

Ingredients:
- 1 cup salted codfish
- 1 cup all-purpose flour
- 1/2 cup water
- 1 small onion, finely chopped
- 2 scallions, chopped
- 1/2 tsp thyme
- 1/4 tsp black pepper
- Oil for frying

Instructions:
1. Soak and rinse the salted codfish, then flake into small pieces.

2. In a bowl, mix flour, thyme, black pepper, onion, and scallions.
3. Gradually add water to form a thick batter, then fold in the flaked codfish.
4. Heat oil in a pan over medium heat. Drop spoonfuls of batter into the hot oil and fry until golden brown.
5. Drain on paper towels and serve hot with a spicy dipping sauce.

3. St. Lucian Bouyon (Hearty Island Soup)
Bouyon is a flavorful, hearty soup that's a staple in St. Lucian cuisine, often made with a mix of meat, dumplings, and fresh vegetables.

Ingredients:
- 1 lb chicken, beef, or pork (cubed)
- 2 green bananas, sliced
- 1 sweet potato, diced
- 1 carrot, sliced
- 1 onion, chopped
- 2 cloves garlic, minced
- 1 sprig thyme
- 1 scotch bonnet pepper (optional)
- 2 cups coconut milk
- Salt and black pepper to taste

Instructions:
1. Brown the meat in a large pot with onions, garlic, thyme, salt, and pepper.
2. Add coconut milk and water, then bring to a boil.

3. Add green bananas, sweet potato, and carrot. Simmer until vegetables are tender.
4. Adjust seasoning and serve hot with crusty bread.

4. Cocoa Tea (St. Lucian Hot Chocolate)
Cocoa tea is a traditional St. Lucian breakfast drink, made from locally grown cocoa sticks and spices. It's rich, comforting, and perfect for starting your day.

Ingredients:
- 1 stick of cocoa (grated)
- 2 cups water
- 1 cup coconut milk
- 1/2 tsp cinnamon
- 1/4 tsp nutmeg
- 1/4 cup sugar (or to taste)

Instructions:
1. In a pot, bring water and grated cocoa to a boil.
2. Add cinnamon and nutmeg, then simmer for 10-15 minutes.
3. Stir in coconut milk and sugar. Adjust sweetness to taste.
4. Strain the tea and serve hot.

5. Rum-Soaked Banana Cake
This moist, flavorful cake combines the sweetness of ripe bananas with the depth of St. Lucian rum. It's a perfect dessert for any island celebration.

Ingredients:
- 3 ripe bananas, mashed
- 1/2 cup St. Lucian rum
- 1 cup sugar
- 1/2 cup butter, softened
- 2 eggs
- 1 tsp vanilla extract
- 1 1/2 cups flour
- 1 tsp baking powder
- 1/4 tsp baking soda
- Pinch of salt

Instructions:

1. Preheat oven to 350°F (180°C). Grease a loaf pan.
2. In a bowl, mix mashed bananas and rum. Set aside for 10 minutes.
3. In a separate bowl, cream butter and sugar until light and fluffy. Add eggs one at a time, then stir in vanilla extract.
4. Mix in the banana-rum mixture.
5. In another bowl, whisk together flour, baking powder, baking soda, and salt. Fold into the wet ingredients.
6. Pour batter into the prepared pan and bake for 45-50 minutes, or until a toothpick comes out clean.
7. Let the cake cool before slicing. Enjoy with a scoop of ice cream or a drizzle of caramel.

Printed in Great Britain
by Amazon